VINTAGE
& spirits
forgotten
COCKTAILS

GLOUCESTER MASSACHUSETTS

QUARRY BOOKS

VINTAGE spirits & forgotten COCKTAILS

FROM THE ALAMAGOOZLUM COCKTAIL TO THE ZOMBIE
80 Rediscovered Recipes and the Stories behind Them

TED HAIGH, a.k.a. DR. COCKTAIL

First published in the United States of America by
Quarry Books, an imprint of
Rockport Publishers, Inc.
33 Commercial Street
Gloucester, Massachusetts 01930-5089
Telephone: (978) 282-9590
Fax: (978) 283-2742
www.rockpub.com

Library of Congress Cataloging-in-Publication Data
Haigh, Ted.
    Vintage spirits and forgotten cocktails : from the alamagoozlum
  cocktail to the zombie : 80 rediscovered recipes and the stories
behind them / Ted "Dr. Cocktail" Haigh.
       p.   cm.
    Includes index.
    ISBN 1-59253-068-0 (pbk.)
    1. Cocktails. I. Title: Vintage spirits and forgotten cocktails. II.
Title.
    TX951.H223 2004
    641.8'74—dc22   2004006730
                                                        CIP

ISBN 1-59253-068-0

10 9 8 7 6 5 4 3 2 1

Design: Moth Design
Layout: Collaborated, Inc.
Additional Art Direction by Ted Haigh.
Photography on pages 21; 24; 30; 32; 34; 36; 38; 40; 42; 44; 49; 50;
    52; 54; 56; 58; 60; 72; 76; 80; 84; 87; 88; 90; 92; 93; 94; 96; 98; 100;
    104; 106; 112; 118; 122; 126; 128 Allan Penn, Photographer/
    C. Dwayne Ridgaway, Stylist.
All other images by Ted Haigh.
Cover images: Allan Penn, Photographer/C. Dwayne Ridgaway, Stylist

Printed in Singapore

Dedicated to David Donovan—
without him, there wouldn't have been a book;
to Rick Corsini—lab partner in all things Cocktail;
and to Nurse Cocktail—partner in all else.

Acknowledgments

Since I started this journey into the overgrown thicket of cocktail research, I've had many a helping hand. Those listed here have done extraordinary service, to my little book and me. Thank you.

Jeff Berry, Gae Buckley, Fernando Castellon, Dale DeGroff, Martin Doudoroff, Carl Ferraro, Colin Field, Roy Finamore, Bill Grimes, Mary Ann Hall, Robert Hess, John Hodgman, Sven Kirsten, Robert McCarthy, Ross McDonald, Tony Ramos, Brian Rea, Gary & Mardee Regan, Steve Remsberg, Chuck Taggart, Mary Linn Wolf, Dave Wondrich, the whole gang from the AOL and Drinkboy drink boards, and to David Hill & Lynn Kneedler, two personal boosters and beloved former teachers.

SEELBACH

SECRET

CHATHAM SPE

VESPER

ALGONQUIN

FRED COLLINS FIZZ

GEORGIA
MINT
JULEP

LEATHERNE

PICON PUNCH

STRAITS SLING

MOTHER-IN-LAW

ALAMAGOOZLUM

MOSCOW M

FOGCUTTER

MILK PUNCH

CONTENTS

Introduction 8
Cocktail Archaeology 10

RECIPES

The Alamagoozlum Cocktail 21
The Jack Rose Cocktail 24
The Fred Collins Fiz 28
Barbara West Cocktail 29
The Jupiter Cocktail 30
The Mother-In-Law Cocktail 32
The Algonquin Cocktail 34
The Avenue Cocktail 36
The Golden Dawn 38
The Twentieth Century Cocktail 40
The Brandy Crusta 42
The Corpse Reviver #2 44
The Modernista 47
Vieux Carré Cocktail 48
Soyer au Champagne 49
The Coffee Cocktail 50
The Delicious Sour 52
The Secret Cocktail 54
Blood and Sand 56
East India Cocktail 58
The Brooklyn Cocktail 59
The French 75 60
The Seelbach Cocktail 62
The Georgia Mint Julep 64
Pink Gin 66
The Income Tax Cocktail 68
Barnum (Was Right) Cocktail 70
The Bebbo Cocktail 71
The Filmograph Cocktail 72
The Aviation 74
Chatham Hotel Special 75
La Floridita Daiquiri 76
The Widow's Kiss 80
The Derby Cocktail 83
The Millionaire Cocktail 84
Knickerbocker a la Monsieur 87

The Monkey Gland 88
The Scoff Law Cocktail 90
The Blackthorn Cocktail 92
The Blinker Cocktail 93
Palm Beach Special 94
Park Avenue Cocktail 95
Pegu Club Cocktail 96
Picon Punch 98
The Calvados Cocktail 100
Pendennis Cocktail 102
Ritz Sidecar 103
Doctor Cocktail 104
Satan's Whiskers Cocktail 106
The Moscow Mule 110
The Communist 112
The Fogcutter 114
Fogcutter (Early) 115
Curaçao Punch 116
Seventh Heaven 117
The Straits Sling 118
The Rose 120
Have a Heart Cocktail 120
Royal Bermuda Yacht Club Cocktail . . 121
The Vesper 122
Crimean Cup á la Marmora 124
Vowel Cocktail 125
Leatherneck Cocktail 126
Lucien Gaudin Cocktail 127
Milk Punch 128
Don the Beachcomber's Zombie 130

Great Old Standards 132
Resource Guide 137
Bibliography 140
About the Author 141
Afterword 142
Index 143

Once upon a midnight dreary, while I pondered, weak and weary
Over many a quaint and curious volume of forgotten lore . . .
—Edgar Allan Poe

Greetings, cocktail archaeologists!

You presumably picked up this treasury because you are intrigued by the concept of the forgotten cocktail and that's what *Vintage Spirits & Forgotten Cocktails* serves up. I'll also include a few old recipes—the great standards, mainly so you can compare them to their brethren. . .the cocktails left behind. As the title suggests, what you'll find here are recipes you'll *never* find in a bar or restaurant. All of these recipes contain ingredients that are currently available. If you can't find them all locally, don't worry, I've provided a Resource Guide in the back of the book to help you have them delivered.

Many twists of history in near and far-flung places have seen wonderful old recipes discarded by the wayside, and it is my goal to see the best of them resurrected. No recipe will suit every person or every situation, but these 80 hand-picked recipes, rarely made today, all deserve revival simply because they are so pleasant to drink. Some are from the nineteenth century, some from the Prohibition era, and some from after World War II, as the golden age of the cocktail was waning. The recipes are retrieved from uncommon sources. Of course, since I was able to find these drinks, they may not be *entirely* forgotten, but you'll rack up quite a bill collecting the rare old bar guides that originally listed them.

If you walk into a bar, order one of the drinks in this book, and the bartender knows how to make it, then that is a bartender well worth noting. In fact, some of these drinks were found carefully penned into old cocktail manuals or on scraps of paper and may *never* have been published. They are true treasures indeed. I promise not to tempt you with recipes containing ingredients (liqueurs or bitters, for instance) that are no longer made. I own 99 percent of all ingredients ever used in any cocktail, but if you can't get it, I won't torture you with it—though I may gripe a bit about its absence if I think it might encourage some farsighted compounder to revive it for the good of all. (With our Internet economy, such a thing is far more viable than ever before.) I will challenge you to search out uncommon ingredients because they are often the lone obstacles that transform popular cocktails into forgotten ones. That said, I will always give you my personal leads as to where these ingredients can be ordered. Some are so good I liken them to secret weapons. (You should be very excited.)

I have had a fascination with cocktails ever since, as a kid, I saw all those cocktail-laden 1930s society movies like the *Thin Man*. It was really all I knew about drinking. Because my parents weren't really drinkers, I only saw Hollywood's iconographic vision of it on the silver screen. One fateful day, hidden away atop a tall bookcase, I came upon an old copy of Patrick Gavin Duffy's *Official Mixer's Manual* (1934). I looked with unrestrained fascination at all the arcane liquor names: Swedish Punsch, Batavia Arrack, Forbidden Fruit, and so many more. With wide eyes I noted the cocktails—the Corpse Reviver, the Monkey Gland, the Bosom Caresser—and the die was cast. I tucked this interest away in my head until I was old enough to act on it, though exactly how that might happen, I did not know.

By the early 1980s, as an adult, still tenacious in my every interest, I began to accumulate old books (like Duffy's) on the subject. I also started acquiring the obscure booze to reproduce those strange old potions. In a few years, I was finally able to sample the primary object of my initial ardor: The Corpse Reviver #2. I found the final ingredient (which ten years later would be so easily located online) after years of searching, and I made the drink. To my amazement, it was the finest thing to ever pass over my palate. I could taste every ingredient. It was subtle, it was fresh, it was complex, and it was delicious. After that, I was a man on a mission. My research and acquisitions continued with renewed vigor.

In the early 1990s, thinking myself alone in these interests, I made my auspicious entry into the fledgling World Wide Web as AgingWino@aol.com. I began humbly answering questions on the AOL Drinks bulletin boards based on my years of research. There *were* kindred spirits out there! At some ego-driven point, I changed my name to Dr. Cocktail, and was immediately asked to become the host of the spirits boards. It was on this stage that I made my (odd) reputation. I got to know such cocktail greats as Gary and Mardee Regan, Dale "King Cocktail" DeGroff, Martin Doudoroff, William Grimes, David Wondrich, Robert "Drinkboy" Hess, Colin Field, and Audrey "Libation Goddess" Saunders. In the intervening years, I have been quoted and referenced in the *New York Times, Esquire, The Malt Advocate, Men's Journal,* and in various books and other media. I became a partner in CocktailDB.com where we try to promote an encyclopedic knowledge of the cocktail and related drink forms.

Vintage Spirits & Forgotten Cocktails is an homage to the great bartenders of the past and the beverages they created, lost in time, but still grand and full of potential. The vintage illustrations, bottles, and cocktail artifacts you see throughout the book are all from my personal collection. They are matched in age to the drinks calling for them. If you have half the fun looking at this book and trying these recipes as I did putting them all together, a great party is about to ensue.

Ted "Dr. Cocktail" Haigh
Los Angeles, California

Cocktail Archaeology

When it comes to cocktails, it's been a wild ride.

Of course, you can *drink* cocktails like perfect ladies and gentlemen if you have a mind to (though the more you consume the harder that will be) but the ride the cocktail itself has taken—whew! I'll give it to you in a blow-by-blow narrative, but first a little quiz. How *long* do you think the cocktail has been around? Since before Prohibition? Pre–World War I? Try again. The venerable and very American cocktail is a minimum of 200 years old.

Trade card, circa 1917

Hell, the *Martini* is more than 100 years old. There is a lot of history there, embedded beneath our cultural skin, when it comes to this roustabout drink form.

The newly minted cocktail first got noticed when Thomas Jefferson was president. It was written up in a newspaper, and not in a particularly

Newspaper nameplate, 1806

positive way. The citation noted what kind of drink it was and then suggested that Democrats who drank them would, under their effects, vote for anyone.

Ah, but the real shocker was not spelled out:

Cocktail napkin, circa 1948

Cocktails were morning drinks. Nobody knows for sure, but I feel certain that they were named cocktails because they were your wakeup call—like a rooster heralding the early morning light.

Now, as much as times change, human nature stays the same. People were largely outraged at the cocktail much as they remain indignant today about morning drinking. Drinking in the morning often means getting over what you were drinking the night before, and that kind of behavior is what they used to call "dissipated." Cocktails were in the realm of sporting men—and by sporting I mean gamblers, hustlers, and protégés of loose women—not baseball fans. And women drinking cocktails? Edgier still.

If you drank a cocktail, you were a little dangerous and therein lay the seeds of its fame. It was the "bad boy" syndrome.

So the cocktail became incrementally more popular while being roundly eschewed

Photograph, 1930

by polite society. In a few years, the avenue to its more general acceptance made itself evident: the historical equivalent of a tailgate party. Sporting men passed the cocktail baton over to actual sportsmen and cocktails began to appear at fox hunts, polo matches, and other cultured (i.e., more moneyed) forms of morning entertainment.

This is the nature of how *all* innovations are eventually deployed as bona fide cultural elements. The new is often shocking merely as a result of our phobic resistance to change. Add to that any more specific tweaking of our societal noses (hair-of-the-dog morning drinking in this case)—and the knee-jerk result is the impression of absolute *scandal*. It happens quite consistently, and there is no better example than in the realm of popular music. Violent reactions were had to all the following genres of music: ragtime, jazz, rock and roll, and rap. Ragtime was considered mindless pabulum;

the rest were perceived as savage incitements to sex or violence.

So it was with cocktails. Gamblers frequented horse tracks, as did high-falutin horse owners and their hoity-toity offspring and sycophants. To the latter, the sour reaction to the cocktail added a dangerous element that they found very attractive. In our capitalistic society, the economic stature of this group incrementally tamed the new drink form by making it fashionable. Still, it would be another 50 years before the cocktail got another big leg up, ironically, against the backdrop of the American Civil War.

What happened between that 1806 newspaper column and 1862 was the integration of the cocktail, through familiarity, into more general acceptance. By this time, it had ceased to be typecast as a morning drink and was consumed at less controversial hours. Still, there were no standards of measurement or ingredients, and no preeminent cocktails—*yet*.

A bartender named Jerry Thomas changed all that when, in 1862, he authored the first bartender's guide ever published.

Suddenly you could get the same whiskey cocktail at one bar as you could across town, or across the country. A slew of other bar books followed. All these books were how-to

Title page, 1862

manuals *by* bartenders *for* bartenders. They were the equivalent of TV repair handbooks. Yeah, the general public could buy them, but. . .why?

They were technical trade manuals. As with other technical writings, they contained many definitions, classifications, and subclassifications. The cocktail was one of those.

Nowadays, we think of practically any beverage made with hard liquor as a cocktail. Not so back then. A Mint Julep wasn't a cocktail; it was a julep. A Sloe Gin Fizz wasn't a cocktail; it was a fizz.

A Singapore Sling wasn't a cocktail; it was a sling. (OK, on this last point I've taken some dramatic license. There *were* slings in those days, but not yet anything called a *Singapore* sling.) There were also crustas, fixes, sangarees, neguses, scaffas, smashes, cobblers, flips, punches, and, oh yes, cocktails, a separate class altogether. (In fact, cocktails were not the first mixed drinks.

Juleps preceded them, as did swizzles, possets, and several others.)

Stereopticon view, circa 1890

By modern standards, all of these would be considered cocktails today, but each one was made either in a slightly different glass, with a particular preparation technique, or contained slightly different ingredients. A julep had crushed (or shaved) ice. A flip had egg in it. A crusta had a sugared rim. Punch had fruit juice and tea. Cocktails were booze of choice, sugar, bitters, maybe a dash of liqueur,

stirred or shaken with ice and strained into a stemmed glass with, perhaps, a fruit peel garnish.

Cocktails had the benefit of utter simplicity. They tasted good and got the job done. Eventually the formerly shunned cocktail cannibalized the other categories. All hail, King Cocktail.

Whoa! Not so fast. There would be a couple bumps in the road before that would happen.

Bump 1: Temperance. This movement bore the mantle of religion, but it was as much sociological. Just as the Civil War was a violent reaction between the agrarian South and the urban North (of which the slavery issue was a potent manifestation of the discord), so alcohol represented the new battleground between factions of people struggling to understand the indigence, homelessness, begging, theft, and what they saw as a moral backsliding—all increasingly evident as the country and world moved inexorably toward city life and industrialization. It was simple human nature that people wanted badly to cast blame at some single person, group, or thing. For the Temperance gang,

Temperance postcard, 19

that was alcohol, sometimes beer, often wine, and *always* hard liquor. Bars and spirits sellers were hardly blameless. Before the 1906 Pure Food and Drugs Act, that bottle of "aged whiskey" might just as likely have contained tea, ether, suphuric acid, and creosote. Carrie Nation, an earlier version of the terrorist, would put a mob together, run into bars, and smash them into smithereens with hammers and her trademark hatchet. Bartenders just loved that.

Bump 2: World War I. Lots of our drinkers shipped off to Europe. Cocktails were not foremost on their minds. There was alcohol rationing all around. When our boys got home, we had another little surprise for them. We were about to enact Bump 3.

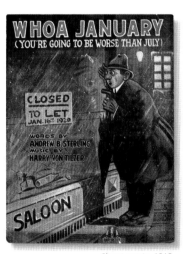
Sheet music, 1919

Bump 3: Prohibition. For a time, the Temperance forces won. Prohibition, during which it was illegal to make or buy alcohol for other than medicinal reasons, was enacted in 1919 and went into effect in January 1920. Few alive today realize just how long Prohibition lasted. When it was finally repealed

at the tail end of 1933, one could finally again order a lawful drink— after 13 long years.

Contrary to the popular wisdom of the time, however, Prohibition was not an obstacle to the increasing ubiquity of the cocktail. . .it was the reason for it.

Nothing is so desired as the thing denied. Prohibition made people want cocktails very, very badly. Because "synthetic" liquor was the easiest to make (quickly distill it, flavor it, bottle it) it was also the easiest to get, and it tasted awful. Cocktails with their melange of flavors were a made-to-order method for disguising the bad hooch. With all hands on deck, people forgot the earlier—now seemingly frivolous—distinctions between types of drinks. This was cultural warfare. All things became cocktails.

Ironic as Prohibition was as a cause célèbre for drinking, so too was the fact that, wheat amidst the chaff, some wonderful cocktail recipes were penned during those 13 years. In fact, Prohibition resulted in a dramatic expansion, both numerically and geographically, of the reign of the cocktail. If you had money (and in the 1920s,

Sheet music, 1920

before the Depression, people did) and you wanted a good drink, you booked steamer passage and took that vacation you'd been promising yourself. You went to Cuba and had Mojitos and Cuba Librés.

Ship cruise schedule, 1930

Hell, virtually all the ocean liners had European registries, and you could start drinking as soon as you were in international waters. The S.S. Kungsholm, for instance, departed from New York City on December 19th 1930 docking in San Juan, Curacao, and Jamaica among other places. The lengthiest port of call was Havana over New Year's. There was even a Kungsholm Cocktail. There were also the British Isles and, of course, Europe. An entire cottage industry sprang up to service the bibulous desires of the expatriate Yank. An important example of this was the UKBG, the United Kingdom Bartenders' Guild, [see page 39]. These chaps were among the most innovative bartenders the world has ever known. Not being able to get some common drink ingredients available in the United States, this group innovated and, out of whole cloth, constructed some incredible cocktail recipes with ingredients of their own. These drinks were rarely seen on American shores either during or after Prohibition, and that's a shame.

Also, largely as a result of journalism *about* Prohibition, we began to see, by the 1920s, a certain shift in who wrote cocktail books. Up to that point, it had always been the bartenders writing for other bartenders

Linebook, circa 1931

and to a lesser extent (as the cocktail's popularity grew) to the general public. On the subject of Prohibition however, the journalist was king. Journalists tore into Prohibition like a political scandal. Given all of their research, they drifted into writing books *on* cocktails. Some transformed their writing into the persuasive patter of a travelogue. Why not? It was more than just drinking now.

New Year's card, 1933

The legal cocktail returned in 1933, its innovative and sophisticated light scarcely dimmed by the shadow of the Great Depression.

With the stock market crash in 1929, talkies the same year, and Prohibition's repeal at the end of

Cocktail book, 1934

1933, the cocktail's appeal had become unequivocal. It was escape; the ultimate fantasy.

At least 18 bar guides and innumerable drink pamphlets were published in the first year following repeal. Their contents were mighty inviting, with a return to good booze and far-away cordials with their strange-sounding names. Movies and radio heralded their return; we were all part of the cocktail club. Why not?

Cocktails symbolized a better world to come, a rainbow around the corner, and, in the bargain, actually produced physical euphoria.

By the 1940s, cocktails were being undermined in a much stealthier manner, though less by design than happenstance. The booze of choice for either cocktails or straight drinking had changed over the years. When America was founded, it was brandy. When that proved expensive and politically imprudent, it became rum. When rum importation proved problematic (the Boston Tea Party might as realistically have been called the Boston Rum Party), we made our own native spirits. The settlers first distilled applejack and later American whiskies of corn, wheat, and rye.

Bottle label, circa 1890

By the birth of the twentieth century, the art of rye and bourbon crafting had become, well, an art. These spirits were hands-down the most popular, straight or mixed, and might well have remained so to this very day but for a series of unfortunate events, some miscalculations, and a lack of forethought. Whiskies require aging. It's what makes them mellow and flavorful. The minimal distilling done during Prohibition dramatically cut down on the stored stocks of aged whiskey, and there was little time to ramp up production for several years' aging following repeal. The 10 years that followed was short time to cure the malaise wrought by the First World War and Prohibition. Then, in number two of a one-two punch, along came the conflict we would come to call World War II. We again endured widespread alcohol rationing. Most of the product went overseas for medical or industrial use.

As the war ended, life (and alcohol supplies) again began, seemingly, to normalize. By the 1940s, there were thousands of published cocktails, in addition to the mere ten written up by Jerry Thomas is 1862.

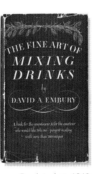

Book jacket, 1948

A third variety of the cocktail writer emerged. With the publication of the seminal book *The Fine Art of Mixing Drinks* by David A. Embury (published by Doubleday), we gained what I call the aficionado class.

Embury was not a bartender. He was not a journalist. He was a lawyer. Just as Wallace Stevens, respected insurance executive, wrote poetry, so Embury wrote his drink book simply because he wanted to.

No axe to grind, he just had something to say about something he enjoyed. This illustrates not mere popularity but also how deeply ingrained the cocktail had become—from being reviled to getting fan mail.

Behind the scenes, however, distillers worried about their meager holdings of aged spirits, and made plans—plans that they instituted before the war and redoubled thereafter. First they started really marketing blended whiskey, which consists of a little bit of aged whiskey and a lot of grain neutral spirits. Neutral spirits require no aging and get no flavoring. They are just raw clear alcohol. Therefore, the liquor companies could double, triple, quadruple, or more the longevity of their aged whiskey stocks as well as the speed at which their product could be produced. It doesn't take much time to distill neutral spirits, and they don't need to age. Add a little aged whiskey, and off to market! To this blended whiskey approach, they then pitched an alternative drinking style: the highball. Take a shot of blended whiskey, add some soda water or ginger ale, and a tall glass with ice cubes. Light! Refreshing! Casual! Modern! So went their mantra.

Liquor pamphlet, circa 1952

Then they *really* did it. They found an ethnic spirit that didn't call for aging, was smooth—unlike straight neutral spirits—and had a very light flavor. This spirit had been a dismal failure in the past. Nobody knew quite what to do with it, and the cocktails calling for it mixed it with gin, which totally covered it up. These execs thought perhaps it could be used *instead* of gin (or whiskey) for a big savings. So again they went into marketing overdrive, and that's how vodka was reborn in America.

Liquor pamphlet, circa 1959

Only they hadn't thought through the consequences. After some initial growing pains, Americans took to the blended whiskey and the vodka alright. In doing so however, they incrementally lost their taste for the flavor of aged alcohol, and really for alcohol at all. Add orange juice to vodka, and it tastes pretty much like orange juice. Society began going for the buzz, not the flavor. This could not have disturbed the liquor companies too much, because, after all, they were selling cheaper product and lots of it.

Consumers didn't stop with vodka. Since they didn't like the flavor of hard alcohol anymore, they turned to wine, which finally after Prohibition began to evolve into a mature industry, as the grapevines in American vineyards themselves matured. They didn't stop there either. Beer got lighter with a lower alcohol percentage. Nor was that the end of it. If people didn't like strong alcohol flavors anymore, why drink at all? The whole subtext of lighter drinks eventually made transparent that which once had been hidden by cultural overlay: alcohol dependency.

Powdered drug envelope circa 1917

By the late 1960s, much of a generation abandoned alcohol in general and cocktails in particular considering them old-fashioned and establishmentarian.

They turned instead to *countercultural* inebriants.

The 1970s were dark years for cocktails. They still carried the scent of conservatism and the staleness of an old-man bar.

Tall, colorful, sweet drinks were in. The classic cocktails withered on the vine, and as the old bartenders retired, their young replacements learned only the bare minimum of old recipes and virtually none of the careful techniques of preparation. Why should they? Nobody ordered any of *that* old stuff anymore. Vodka-based, weak, (or disguised Mickey Finn–strong) sweet, and fruity—that was the 1970s.

The 1980s saw the beginning of a massive downsizing and global consolidation of the liquor industry. Brands died, with whole varieties of liqueurs either irretrievable from a lack of distribution (the new conglomerates wanted only the most profitable brands) or simply defunct victims of their owners' scheming—and the new American taste bud.

Then, toward the end of the 1980s, a curious thing happened. The pendulum that swung so ponderously and far from us in its sweep that it erased itself from memory began an inching return.

I believe it was in one of the mid-priced, national hotel chains in the Midwest where I first recognized the seeds of the rebirth of the cocktail. I caution that what follows is rank theorization on my part, but I was there, I saw the menu, and I believe it. I think it went down something like this: A food and beverage manager (hypothetically) says:

"Hey, I have an idea. I bet this new generation of drinkers would really get into cocktails if we could just get them past the fuddy-duddy name. They wrinkle their noses at 'cocktails,' but they perk up at 'martinis.' They are nostalgic for their vision of the 1950s martini parties they've seen in old movies. Say 'cocktail' and they think geezer bar. Say 'martini' and they get this image of clean, retro sophistication. Only problem is, it's likely none of this crowd has actually ever *had* a real martini, and I bet if they did, it would knock 'em on their ass. WAY too strong. They'd run away screaming. So I say this: Let's mix a little vodka and some liqueur, shaken and strained in a stemmed cocktail glass, and call it a fill-in-the-blank Martini.

"Hey look! They're drinking it! They like it! Let's add some fruit juice this time and do a whole menu of them. Make 'em big. Little drinks will seem stingy.

"Man, these are selling like hotcakes. Let's rename a bunch of those old cocktails 'martinis.' You want to make one with milk in it? Go ahead! Anything goes now!"

So it went.

By the early 1990s there was a definite resurgent nostalgia for the trappings of cocktail culture.

In the 1960s, the oh-so wrongheaded martini, mainly vodka on the rocks, ruled. Finally, by 1990, we were beginning to witness a wide-scale return to the genuine methods of serving cocktails, sans ice, in stemware. Liquor companies were also looking back. They noted that people were drinking less, but perhaps they'd pay more to drink better. Soon Scotch, the likes of which we'd *never* seen much on these shores, began to appear. (The single malt Scotches were always preferred in Scotland.) It occurred to Kentucky distillers that *all* Bourbon was single malt by law, and perhaps it was time to again engage the tastes the U.S.

consumer for real domestic whiskey. It wasn't long before American whiskies of a quality not seen since the end of Prohibition (and now possibly better) were again on the shelves. The same thing has happened for virtually all spirits: tequila, rum, even vodka. As the spirits improved, drinkers became more sophisticated about what makes a good cocktail (and, yes, the term has been returned to us—with a vengeance.) The bars were again stocked, and the bartenders again waved shakers.

But the utter lack of sophistication underlying the quazi-classic approach to *cocktail* preparation brought on its own problems. Drinks were still sweet and too large to maintain the proper chill. Likewise they virtually assured a drunken hangover. Bartenders still thought they were cool waving a vermouth bottle near an inverted road cone of vodka and putting it away. Although adept at wielding trendy proprietary liqueurs in cocktails, they'd largely lost the ability to use the generic mainstays of old, like crème de cacao, apricot brandy, or sloe gin. It is still the rare bartender who knows how to shake or stir a drink correctly—which is to say long enough or with enough ice. I also long for the day when no bar erroneously believes it is acceptable to use vile, artificial "sweet and sour mix" in lieu of fresh-squeezed fruit juice, sweetened to taste with a touch of simple sugar syrup. Moreover, the quality of many modern recipes is mediocre and uninspired. Bar tending is not always seen as a profession anymore. In the nineteenth century, temperance notwithstanding, the proud bartender was considered on par with a fine chef, a creative professional of caliber. Often today it is merely a temp job between other professions.

We, as modern consumers, also still have work to do. As a culture, we are quickly forgetting how to gain acquired tastes.

If something tastes bitter or sharp it is bypassed for an easier-to-contemplate taste sensation. The majority of modern drinks are designed and produced to utterly hide any tang of alcohol, much less the sharp piquant acquired taste of a gin— and it's not just gin we're talking about either. It's brandy, whiskey, and tequila, too. I urge you to acquire challenging tastes. To *really* appreciate the forgotten cocktails celebrated in this book (and to add finds of your own), a sophisticated palette will be of great benefit.

Learn to savor the essence of rum, gin, brandy, and whiskey. Vodka cocktails will never teach you anything.

Margaritas are today what the Mai Tai became 30 years ago. The tropical potions of the Tiki/Polynesian drink movement began seven decades ago as carefully crafted, festive punches that packed a punch but were rife with hidden, persuasive flavors. In the intervening years, the Mai Tai became a generic orange catch-all for any fruity-sweet sucker punch in a bucket. You may have never tasted a real one. And it's a fair bet you may never have had a proper Margarita either. The sweet-and-sour mix in a contemporary margarita combines with the generous portion of triple sec to make a drink as tart and flavor-dangerous as sweet lemonade. They taste "good" like the candied soda pop we were accustomed to as children.

The original Margarita was actually a cocktail, probably the last classic cocktail from the golden age. It was a small drink,

shaken with ice, strained, and served up in a martini glass.

It contained no sweet and sour mix; it didn't need it. It was simply a potion of reposado tequila, Cointreau, and fresh lime juice. You could taste *everything* in this drink, and if it was too sour you could adjust down the lime. Too strong? Add less tequila. Too sweet? Cut back on the Cointreau. It was easy, and with no disgusting, preservative-imbued sweet and sour mix. It is a delicious drink this way, as was its father the Sidecar and its granddaddy the Brandy Crusta. Now that we once again have a solid foundation for correct cocktail construction, it is time to grow and mature with our ever-increasing knowledge. Drinking vodka cocktails is fine, but the best experiences in our lives are challenges we've surmounted—and learning to love and appreciate complex, richly flavored cocktails ranks right up there.

For better or worse, this is where the cocktail's wild ride has left us today. We have bars stocked with great spirits. Bartenders once again shake drinks and serve them in stemmed cocktail glasses.

There is learning and growth going on all around. For all its limitations, the cocktail has indeed enjoyed a rebirth, and my fervent hope is that the rediscovered cocktails in this book contribute in some small way to its future advancement and maturation.

The final element of this equation is the Internet. Many of the formerly hard-to-find ingredients once used in cocktails can now be acquired over the Web. The depth of research material available on such websites as Webtender, iDrink, the

Liquor pamphlet, circa 1940

About.com cocktail boards, ArdentSpirits.com, Drinkboy.com, Esquire.com, KingCocktail.com, and our own CocktailDB.com make getting recipes, definitions, advice, and history easy—though verification of facts from non-online sources remains essential.

Let us always challenge ourselves to new experiences, while never neglecting the oft-glorious contributions of the past.

RECIPES

The Alamagoozlum Cocktail

$^1/_2$ egg white
2 ounces ($^1/_2$ gill, 6 cl) genever gin
2 ounces ($^1/_2$ gill, 6 cl) water
$1^1/_2$ ounces ($^1/_3$ gill, 4.5 cl) Jamaica rum
$1^1/_2$ ounces ($^1/_3$ gill, 4.5 cl) yellow or green Chartreuse
$1^1/_2$ ounces ($^1/_3$ gill, 4.5 cl) *Gomme* syrup (This is glorified sugar water. You can make
   it yourself, but it is cheap. I suggest ordering some from Fee Bros. They call
   theirs Rock Candy Syrup. If you follow this advice, cut the quantity in half—
   $^3/_4$ ounce [$^1/_6$ gill, 2 cl]. They really supersaturate their solution.)
$^1/_2$ ounce ($^1/_8$ gill, 1.5 cl) orange Curaçao
$^1/_2$ ounce ($^1/_8$ gill, 1.5 cl) Angostura bitters

Shake very, *very* hard and long in a large iced cocktail shaker and serve tremulously
into several previously chilled cocktail glasses. As configured, you will get about 3
cocktails out of this recipe, but—to you neophytes out there—you really can't
divide an egg white into even halves, so you're either going to risk messing with the
classic recipe or you'll have to make *six* of 'em! No matter, gather two or three close
friends 'round. You'll want seconds. For specific directions (and justifications) for
using egg white, see the Delicious Sour (page 52).

The banner year of 1939 saw not only the futuristic wonder of the New York World's Fair but also the publication of a book to delight all cocktail explorers, a book unlike any other before or since. Whereas the Fair looked to a glorious future, this tome looked back to travel glories redolent of the Orient Express. However, each stop in *this* travelogue was punctuated by a cocktail. *The Gentleman's Companion*, or *Around the World with Jigger, Beaker and Flask* (1939) was authored by one Charles H. Baker, Jr. He was an editor for *Town & Country* and wrote for *Gourmet*, *Esquire*, and other magazines.

1946 leather-bound limited edition

He wrote *The Gentleman's Companion* in a sly nineteenth-century style calculated to frame each recipe in glorious, mysterious adventure. Not all of his drinks really stood up to the effective presentation, but those that did were real finds, back stories and all.

Such was the case with the Alamagoozlum Cocktail, or as Baker titled it, "J. Pierpont Morgan's Alamagoozlum: the Personal Mix Credited to that Financier, Philanthropist, & Banker of a Bygone Era."

This cocktail breaks common rules of sensible drink making. It contains an inordinately long list of ingredients, including a horrendously large jolt (½ ounce [⅛ gill, 1.5 cl]) of Angostura bitters. Oh, but this potion supercedes such rules! It's quite a production, but well worth it.

If there are any questions why this is a forgotten cocktail, I'm guessing you dipped into the genever early. As with all the uncommon ingredients cited herein, you'll find leads to the genever, the *Gomme* syrup, the Chartreuse, and so on, in the appendix of this book. I don't really know if Chas Baker visited all the places he wrote about, just as it is by no means clear whether J. P. Morgan sipped this ambrosial mixture before his demise in 1912. As the great cartoonist and philosopher Abner Dean once wrote, however, "Don't think—Dream."

Chartreuse bottle from the cellar of J. P. Morgan circa 1900; Hiram Walker orange Curacao circa 1956; copper cocktail shaker circa 1917; Mar-Sé simple syrup circa 1940; Angostura bitters circa 1912; genever gin circa 1902; Jamaican Red Heart rum circa 1945. Genever was Dutch gin and was a different animal than London dry gin. It was made in a pot still and was quite aromatic. The bottle, here, is actually an American-produced genever type gin. This type of imitation was rampant in the spirits industry before laws were enacted to curtail it.

The Jack Rose Cocktail

1½ ounces (⅓ gill, 4.5 cl) applejack
Juice of ½ lime (or lemon—about 1 ounce [¼ gill, 3 cl])
2 or more dashes of real pomegranate grenadine (simple)

Shake well in an iced cocktail shaker, strain into a cocktail glass, and garnish with a lime (or lemon) wedge.

There are three time-worn stories as to how the Jack Rose got its name. (1) It is made with apple*jack*, and it is *rose* colored. (2) A double entendre on the name Jacqueminot Rose, or Jacque Rose, of which Jack Rose is a corruption and with which the drink is color coordinated. This was the firmly held theory of Albert Stevens Crockett, journalist, who wrote of it in his 1931 history-with-recipes of the old pre-

Prohibition Waldorf Astoria bar. Though it is not completely true, this particular rose variety is said to be thornless, and it must be admitted that, likewise, the drink is certainly smooth, not sharp. (3) It was named after a gangster—hit man who was embroiled in an early century murder trial of some notoriety. You can't put it past bartenders to name a drink after current events. That's why we are all drinking Lindberghs, Sacco-Vanzettis, and Simpsons (light on the OJ, please) today. Nah, I vote for #1. Sometimes things are *just* as they seem.

Mainly, I want to discuss the Jack Rose as a launching pad for my praise of its primary constituent, applejack or apple jack.

DRINK NOTES

Recipes, even early ones, differ on whether to use lime or lemon juice in this drink. I've had both, and they are different, but both excellent. Earlier guides seem to prefer lime; later guides, like the back of the applejack bottle, opt for lemon. I'm going to courageously come down right in the middle. I like either or.

Insist on real pomegranate grenadine for your Jack Roses—and all drinks that call for grenadine. Some of the most prevalent brands *don't* contain pomegranate, and it isn't real grenadine without it. After all, the word "grenadine" is French diminutive for pomegranate. I'll recommend Fee Bros. American Beauty Grenadine made in exotic Rochester, New York. Angostura also makes a very good one. See the Resource Guide, page 137, for details.

This is a very silky drink, as profound as it is simple. It is largely forgotten because of its deeply historic, yet obscure base liquor.

Copper cocktail shaker circa 1930s; Nuyens grenadine circa 1938; Captain Applejack apple brandy circa 1939; The playbill is presenting the 1931 Warner Bros. Vitaphone production of the same name

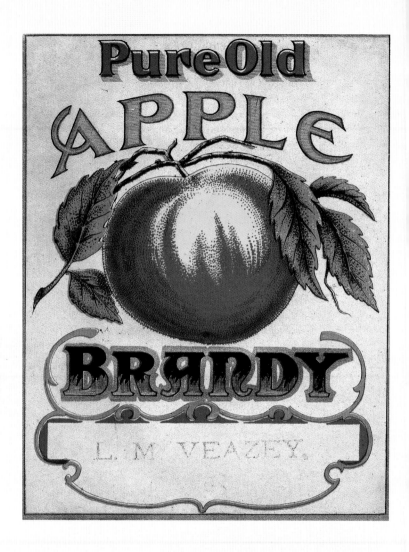

APPLEJACK

Applejack was the first natively distilled spirit in the colonies that would become the United States. Before we made rum, corn likker, or other whiskies, we had applejack, which is a distillate of plentiful hard apple cider. This fruit base makes applejack officially a brandy, but it tastes more like an apple whiskey, and that's largely the way it was used. It's a bit harsher than Calvados, the classic apple brandy from France, but that is to its advantage. It asserts itself where Calvados lays back and remains mellow. Another way of putting it is that in any cocktail calling for Calvados you can substitute applejack. It may make the drink less subtle, but it will work. The reverse is not true. Try a Jack Rose with Calvados. It entirely lacks zing. Applejack, in most areas, was supplanted by whiskey in the nineteenth century. There used to be a number of applejack distillers in Pennsylvania and New Jersey—the places it always called home, right up into the 1930s. Now all are gone save one.

In most industries, having one company gobble up all its competitors would smack of monopolist behavior. Not so with Laird & Co. of Scobeyville, NJ, though. As other applejack distillers faltered—Spea's, Hildick's, Hickory Town's Captain Applejack—Laird bought 'em up. I look upon this as preservation of an American tradition. Besides, no one company or family is more bonded to applejack than Laird's.

William Laird made his first batch of applejack in 1698. His grandson Robert Laird gave their recipe for applejack to George Washington! Grandsons of his built the plant in Scobeyville, and the Laird Company is still on that real estate today. Before the 1950s, most commercial brands called their product apple brandy, as did Laird. "Applejack" was really just a slang term, which eventually became an official designation—a blended variation of apple brandy with neutral spirits and a dash of apple wine. Laird & Co still makes both the straight and blended products, and both are wonderful in cocktails.

In 1991, I wanted to get an image of a 1940s Laird's apple brandy bottle for

Laird's Apple Brandy pamphlet, circa 1934

my research archives. I called Laird & Co. A very nice lady answered the phone, and I asked if they had any old 1940s bottles hanging around I could have or photograph. The conversation went something like this:

"Oh, you'll need to be speaking to Larrie. Hold the line." I heard, "Larrie, pick up the line!" and then some background commotion to the effect of "how do you work this new phone system" and finally "Hello, this is Larrie Laird." My jaw dropped. I said "Larrie

LAIRD as in William Laird, Robert Laird, George Washington, LAIRD???!" He said modestly, "That's me." I was astounded. I again made my pitch, and there was a pause. . ."Well," he said, "we have an old jug on the mantelpiece over here, we could just send it to you." Larrie was willing to send me a family artifact just because I asked. I thanked him profusely and told him I'd consider it. I've not spoken with him since; it was just *too* much responsibility—I couldn't do it. But I'll always love Laird & Co. for that. Thank you, Larrie Laird!

Applejack is well distributed in New York, but just try to find it in Los Angeles bars. I know of only two places that carry it, and I'm Dr. Cocktail! It is generally available in liquor stores, and I hope you go out, get some (it isn't at all expensive), and encourage your local bars to carry it. It is a wonderful, underappreciated ingredient.

The Fred Collins Fiz

2 ounces ($\frac{1}{2}$ gill, 6 cl) Bourbon or rye whiskey
$\frac{1}{2}$ ounce ($\frac{1}{8}$ gill, 1.5 cl) simple syrup
Juice of 1 fresh lemon
$\frac{1}{2}$ a glass of shaved (or finely crushed) ice
1 teaspoon orange Curaçao
6 ounces ($1\frac{1}{2}$ gill, 18 cl) lemonade

Mix all in an iced cocktail shaker, except the Curaçao and lemonade, and shake. Strain into a large bar glass, and add the Curaçao. Pour the lemonade into a collins glass, and add the contents of the bar glass into it.

"The Celebrated Collins Drink is fizzing stuff, only I should be glad if our caterers would agree what it is to be perpetually named. One barkeeper calls it a John Collins—another Tom Collins. There are also Harry and Fred, all members of the same family. I prefer to call mine the **Fred Collins Fiz."**

". . .and drink while lively to the health of the Collins family—whose name you may take in vain for about fifty popular drinks—from brandy, rum, Bourbon, old rye, gin, etc., etc."

Everything you read above about this drink is transcribed verbatim from the *New Guide for the Hotel, Bar, Restaurant, Butler, & Chef* by Bacchus & Cordon Bleu, London, 1885.

Do we see here the precursor to the Lynchburg lemonade? More to the point, it is evident that consternation (and a dash of derision) over new drink trends is nothing new.

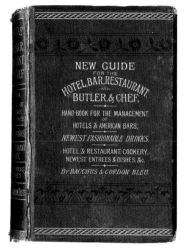

Barbara West Cocktail

⸙

2 ounces (½ gill, 6 cl) gin
1 ounce (¼ gill, 3 cl) sherry
½ ounce (⅛ gill, 1.5 cl) fresh lemon juice
1 small dash Angostura bitters

Shake in an iced cocktail shaker, and strain into a cocktail glass. Garnish with a lemon twist.

⸙

The sad but certain truth is that some drinks, even very good ones, simply were not well named. The Barbara West (sometimes just called the Barbara, although there was also a Barbara East) hardly rolls off the tongue, though there are worse examples, such as the Pansy Blossom or the Fluffy Ruffles. How about the Weesuer or the Bich's Special? Again, no one was trying to be funny here, any more than they were when they christened the Diarrhea Mixture. Still, they can't have done much for their popularity. The Barbara West was the same drink as the euphoniously named Creole Cocktail, but with the agreeable addition of bitters. This provides every justification for fervently ordering a Creole with bitters. I won't stop you.

DRINK NOTES

When I make the Babs W. for myself, I prefer an amontillado sherry. It's dry, pleasantly nutty, and not at all sweet; the perfect approach for this Martini-like cocktail. I also mix the gin and sherry in 4 to 1 proportions—even more like a Martini—which is called a Gordon's Cocktail and is also excellent.

Burnett's Gin circa 1934; Sherry circa 1917; Hazel Atlas bitters bottle circa 1940s; cocktail shaker circa 1930s

The Jupiter Cocktail

1½ ounces (⅓ gill, 4.5 cl) gin
¾ ounce (⅙ gill, 2 cl) dry vermouth
1 teaspoon Parfait Amour
1 teaspoon orange juice

Shake in an iced cocktail shaker, and strain into a cocktail glass.

I first encountered this drink in a great little bar guide published in 1937 by a
Chicago liquor store named Marco's. As a cocktail historian, you'll often turn
up these old recipes at some undetermined point in their "life cycles." When I
make this drink, I always pull down my copy of *The How and When* by Hyman Gale
and Gerald F. Marco, though my cocktail archaeology has determined that Marco's
likely got the recipe from the Patrick Gavin Duffy's *1934 Official Mixer's Manual.* Duffy
probably got it, through his publisher, from Harry Craddock's *Savoy Cocktail Book* in
1930, and Harry most certainly extracted it from another Harry. . .Harry McElhone
in his first book, *Harry of Ciro's ABC of Mixing Cocktails,* published in 1923!

They all saw fit to print the Jupiter's recipe, and right they were; it is, in my view, the finest use of the arcane nineteenth-century liqueur Parfait Amour ever created. You see, Parfait Amour (which translates as "perfect love") was always considered to be a dainty woman's liqueur. It was a pretty purple color and it tasted like the delicate combination of grape jelly beans and marshmallows. Who would have thought that this demure cordial would be so bossy? Parfait Amour, like the more flagrant absinthe and pastis, would, with a heavy pour, absolutely take over a drink—and not in a good way. I love the stuff, but then I *know* it's like a machine gun; I don't aim it just anywhere and I squeeze the trigger very, very carefully.

DRINK NOTES

Simple recipe, right? Well, as you might gather, the Jupiter requires (more than any other cocktail in this book) exact measurements. Got lab equipment? I use a $1\frac{1}{2}$ to $1\frac{3}{4}$ ounce ($\frac{1}{6}$ to $\frac{1}{3}$ gill, 2 to 4.5 cl) jigger and kitchen measuring spoons. No, your coffee spoon will not do. Unlike the Corpse Reviver #2 (see page 44), an overpour won't obviously ruin the drink—but it'll make it disappointing to the point you'll wonder what all the fuss was about. The color won't help. Once you've combined all the constituents, it'll look like gray ashes. If you measure it correctly, you'll get an empyrean flavor like none you've ever experienced and a balance that'll make you want more than one. But the color still won't be anything you'll want to paint your house.

Parfait Amour isn't common, but, thanks to Marie Brizard, it is still made and it is available. In Europe, Bols still makes it too. The Parfait Amour, the devilish mixing required, and the big belt of vermouth made this a natural forgotten cocktail. Be brave. Try it for the flavor.

Garnier Parfait Amour circa 1934; Calvert gin circa 1940; Planter's Cocktail Peanut tin circa 1950; cocktail shaker and glasses circa 1940s

The Mother-In-Law Cocktail

1 teaspoon Peychaud Bitters
1 teaspoon Angostura bitters
1 teaspoon Amer Picon (substitute Torani Bitters)
½ ounce (⅛ gill, 1.5 cl) orange Curaçao
½ ounce (⅛ gill, 1.5 cl) simple syrup
½ ounce (⅛ gill, 1.5 cl) maraschino liqueur
9 ounces (2¼ gill, 27 cl) Bourbon

Shake in an iced cocktail shaker, and strain into cocktail glasses. Makes 3 drinks.

A while back, traveler, gourmand, and cocktail aficionado Chuck Taggart sent an email my way from a fellow named Brooks Baldwin who, as it turned out, had discovered a bona fide forgotten cocktail. Most of the drinks in this book are uncommon, and you'd be hard put to order any in a bar without more than a little explanation. Two drinks I offer are, however, genuinely unearthed from oblivion— this one and the Seelbach (page 62).

This is what Mr. Baldwin said: "My grandmother (born in New Orleans in 1895) inherited the recipe from her mother-in-law shortly before the beginning of the first World War. As specified in the original recipe, my grandmother concocted this libation by the quart and stored it in an antique lead crystal decanter. Informed that science had linked lead crystal to lead poisoning, my grandmother said: 'It's a pretty bottle, so hush.'" The unnamed cocktail recipe was found crammed in his grandmother's recipe box.

DRINK NOTES

The interesting combination of ingredients did not initially recall any specific cocktail, but there was a lingering sense of familiarity, so I set to work rooting out similar concoctions. It sounded a bit like a Brooklyn Cocktail, which contained rye or Bourbon, dry vermouth, Amer Picon, and Maraschino liqueur. Close, but no cigar. As it would turn out, the recipe was a genuine variation of one old classic recipe—itself a variation: the Zazarac Cocktail (not to be confused with the Sazerac), a cocktail rarely made in its own right. It usually (if "usually" can be used here in any way) contains rye, rum, anisette, sugar syrup, Angostura bitters, orange bitters, and absinthe (or pastis). Despite some ingredients in common, the stew of other constituents did not bring it immediately to mind.

Serious bartenders have always made their own personal lists of recipes, from before Jerry Thomas on. I found the missing link in the back of a 1930s bartender's pocket notebook, constructed by one Chas. O. Gash of the Texas Company (which became Texaco). The last two recipes, neatly hand-typed, were his two variations of the Zazarac. The first contained rye, sweet vermouth, Amer Picon, Curaçao, sugar, and absinthe. The second contained whiskey, Amer Picon, Peychaud and orange bitters, and absinthe. When I rolled these recipes together, I could achieve something quite similar to Brooks's newly unearthed formula. Even so, the lack of absinthe and the necessity of combining the recipes unevenly made me feel that his drink needed its own name. Brooks complied with the mother-in-law cocktail title, and Chuck made up the first batch.

Note that this was intended as a bottled cocktail, kept and served from a decanter as a port or brandy might be. I reduced the recipe without getting into really odd measures. By original measure, the drink was to contain 2½ teaspoons Peychaud's bitters, 2½ teaspoons Angostura bitters, 2½ teaspoons Amer Picon, 1½ ounces (⅓ gill, 4.5 cl) orange Curaçao, 1½ ounces (⅓ gill, 4.5 cl) simple syrup, 1½ ounces (⅓ gill, 4.5 cl) maraschino (it said "syrup" but we are all sure "liqueur" was meant). Mix, then fill a quart bottle with Bourbon to make the quart.

The Algonquin Cocktail

1½ ounces (⅓ gill, 4.5 cl) rye
¾ ounce (⅙ gill, 2 cl) dry vermouth
¾ ounce (⅙ gill, 2 cl) pineapple juice

Shake in an iced cocktail shaker, and strain into a cocktail glass.
Your Doctor prefers this one ungarnished and unvarnished.

amed for the New York hotel that was once home to the Algonquin Round Table—both the piece of furniture and the archetypes of ruthless literary cleverness. Dorothy Parker, Robert Benchley, George Kaufman, and Edna Ferber were among the latter. The hotel is still there, but alas, the table, the wits, and the original bar are all long gone. Thank the star-speckled heavens we still have the drink, though I doubt many in the Viscous Circle consumed it.

1936 liquor pamphlet

Old Bridgeport Rye Whiskey dated—distilled 1917 and bottled 1924 (making it, per the National Prohibition Act "medicinal" spirits); dry vermouth circa 1940; cocktail shaker—Forman Bros. circa 1936; *Tales of a Wayward Inn* (the story of the Algonquin hotel by its owner/manager Frank Case) 1938

The Avenue Cocktail

1 ounce (¼ gill, 3 cl) Bourbon
1 ounce (¼ gill, 3 cl) Calvados
1 ounce (¼ gill, 3 cl) passion fruit juice (or nectar)
1 dash real pomegranate grenadine
1 dash orange flower water

Shake in an iced cocktail shaker, and strain into a cocktail glass. Garnish with a carnation boutonnière.

The delicious Avenue is, vitally, from the esteemed *Café Royal Cocktail Book* (1937). You can read more about the book and the group behind it under the Golden Dawn (page 38) and the Twentieth Century (page 40) recipes.

Passionola circa 1930s; Old Crow circa 1900; Pere Magloire Calvados circa 1940; Louis Glunz Grenadine circa 1937

DRINK NOTES

Oddly, the biggest impediment to making this delicious cocktail is a rare fruit juice! For whatever reason, passion fruit juice (or even nectar) is mighty hard to find. There are leads in the Resource Guide, but I also will advise that the drink *can* be made with passion fruit syrup which, thanks to Trader Vic, is cheaper and easier to locate. If you choose this route, the Avenue will still taste great, but I'd substitute a dash of lemon juice for the grenadine, as the cocktail will suddenly get a lot sweeter.

The Golden Dawn

¾ ounce (⅙ gill, 2 cl) Calvados
¾ ounce (⅙ gill, 2 cl) dry gin
¾ ounce (⅙ gill, 2 cl) Cointreau
¾ ounce (⅙ gill, 2 cl) apricot-flavored brandy
   (Marie Brizard's Apry is a fine choice)
¾ ounce (⅙ gill, 2 cl) orange juice

Shake like crazy in an iced cocktail shaker, and strain into a cocktail glass.
Drop a stemless cherry with no pick into the drink as garnish. Dribble a little
real pomegranate grenadine through the drink. Do not stir.

Members of the United Kingdom Bartenders Guild authored three of the drinks included in this book. The Golden Dawn is one of them. This group of talented, resourceful bartenders took up where their American brethren left off during Prohibition and created some fantastic drinks. There was something about the cocktails they created that was subtly different than American drinks of the day, which, by the 1920s, already had more than 100 years of tradition informing their chemistry. Sometimes the framework of tradition makes rigid that which ought to remain flexible. The Englishmen in the UKBG, having no such history, were quite flexible and their cocktails seemed somehow more modern than did those of their American counterparts. This is a generalization, because no one on Earth was or is immune from throwing together a bad drink, then *or* now, but this group used interesting flavors, fruits, colors, and spirits the Americans didn't think of. The best of those results were utterly delicious. The Golden Dawn added the element of simplicity. Equal parts make this an easy drink to mix.

DRINK NOTES

This drink is one where orange juice from a carton works fine. Using fresh squeezed, however, makes the cocktail a bit livelier and more tart. You might also substitute good old American applejack for the Calvados. The drink suffers no ill effects from it and is, in fact, great either way you mix it. In the United States, both components are less than common, but both are available and are excellent quarry for the true cocktail archaeologist (as is Apry). One last note regarding my comments about tradition and rigidity: The cocktail resurgence we find ourselves in (or more correctly the gap between the golden era and the resurgence) has again moved us several steps away from hidebound tradition, and a few truly innovative cocktails have resulted. If we are able to innovate *and* pick selectively from the innovations of the past, imagine the choices we will have!

The Twentieth Century Cocktail

I½ ounces (⅓ gill, 4.5 cl) gin
¾ ounce (⅙ gill, 2 cl) Lillet Blanc
¾ ounce (⅙ gill, 2 cl) light crème de cacao
¾ ounce (⅙ gill, 2 cl) fresh lemon juice

Shake in an iced cocktail shaker, and strain into a cocktail glass. Garnish with a lemon twist.

At first blush, this drink appears to be a mere variation of the Corpse Reviver #2 (page 44), and by ingredient tabulation, it certainly is. On the other hand, a good 40 years stretched between the inventions of the two drinks, and their flavors are quite individual. The original Corpse Reviver was a product of the tentative experimentation of nineteenth century mixology. The Twentieth Century Cocktail, however, was squarely rooted in the post-Prohibition 1930s, named as much for the train, the Twentieth Century Limited, as for the century, already a third over.

The first publication of the recipe was in the *Café Royal Bar Book* of 1939, a year after the celebrated new streamlined train debuted. With this cocktail, I believe we now have a firm idea of exactly what Art Deco tastes like.

DRINK NOTES

The *Café Royal Bar Book* was the unofficial recipe guide of the United Kingdom Bartender's Guild. This drink and the Golden Dawn (page 38) serve as sumptuous samples of the group's artistry.

I hesitate to describe in detail the flavors of the cocktails in this book, preferring instead that each be a revelation to you. I'm going to make an exception here simply because this cocktail's subtle flavor is so uncommon. It goes down like light, zingy lemonade, but in the aftertaste there is an ethereal *sense* of chocolate. It's an amazing experience you won't want to miss. Gary Regan, with his lovely cocktail-scribing wife (they form the first real cocktailian dynasty), has authored a half dozen influential books on the subject. I asked him what his favorite lost cocktail wa.s . .and this is it. (He then graciously reminded me that I introduced him to it!)

Tip: If the chocolate flavor is too pronounced from the onset, cut back slightly on the cacao.

THE *New* 20ᵀᴴ CENTURY LIMITED
NEW YORK-16 hours-CHICAGO
NEW YORK CENTRAL SYSTEM

The Brandy Crusta

Cut a lemon in half.

Pare the full peel off half, and squeeze the juice from the lemon.

Moisten glass rim with lemon juice, and dip it in bar or table sugar.

Insert a lemon peel into the glass.

Mix in a cocktail shaker of crushed ice:

2 ounces (½ gill, 6 cl) cognac (Hennessy works well)

1 teaspoon orange Curaçao (Marie Brizard is best)

½ teaspoon fresh lemon juice

1 dash of Boker's Bitters (This is a long defunct brand. A formula for making your own is in the back of this book. In later years, Angostura was used, so feel free.)

Shake, and strain into a prepared glass. Add 1 small lump of ice, and serve.

The fourth engraving in the first bartenders' guide ever published is of the Brandy Crusta. In "Professor" Jerry Thomas's 1862 *Bar-Tender's Guide*, he calls the crusta class of drink an improvement on the cocktail. Time has not proven him right. What the crusta *was* was a fancy embellishment on the cocktail. It does live on, however, as what I like to call an "ancestor recipe." The Brandy Crusta begat the Sidecar Cocktail, which in turn begat the Margarita.

Among some cocktail historians, those are fighting words, but let's look at the history: Joe Santini invented the crusta drink form in New Orleans in the years closely preceding Thomas's book. He took the basic cocktail formula (spirits, bitters, water) and added a skirt of fruit peel, a liqueur, and its namesake crust of sugar on the rim of the glass. It was festive and added just a dash of showmanship to the utilitarian cocktail. It was also quite tasty, and it remained popular into the twentieth century and available even after Prohibition.

Speaking of Prohibition, the Sidecar was unquestionably the most famous product of those years. Harry McElhone first published the recipe in 1922 (there is a book with a 1904 copyright that lists it, but it was evidently a 1920s reprint) and credited its invention to a bartender named McGarry, who was then working at an American bar, a bar that served American-style drinks mainly during U.S. Prohibition, in London. Years later in 1947, drink book author David Embury would say the drink was invented by a friend of his at a bar in Paris during World War I. It probably wasn't the Ritz, or Frank Meier would have claimed it in his 1936 book, which he did not. It's even a little before Prohibition, and we can assume perhaps that the aforementioned McGarry might have done a stint in Paris, only later to end up in London with his Sidecar. Or maybe Embury just made an assumption.

There's our premise, now consider this: In those years, the bars were definitely serving the popular crustas. It stands to reason that the inventor of the Sidecar had made any number of Brandy Crustas previously. The original Jerry Thomas Brandy Crusta recipe is published here.

So basically the Brandy Crusta contained brandy, lemon juice, orange Curaçao, and bitters. The Sidecar contained brandy, lemon juice, and Cointreau—a proprietary orange liqueur made with Curaçao oranges. No bitters were used, and it had no lemon skirt, but tellingly it adopted the Crusta trademark—the sugared rim. More quickly and easily served, the Sidecar, son of Crusta, remains popular to this day. Even more popular is the Margarita. The original recipe mirrors the Sidecar but substitutes tequila for brandy, lime for lemon juice, and a salt-crusted rim for sugar. Both had Cointreau, all proportions were exactly the same, and both were shaken and strained. (Bars would later cheap out with triple sec instead of Cointreau and substitute disgusting sweet and sour mix for fresh juice in both drinks. On-the-rocks and frozen versions also came later.)

I rest my case, but do try the original. It is the most "modern" tasting drink from the first mixed drink guide ever.

The Corpse Reviver #2

1 ounce (¼ gill, 3 cl) gin
1 ounce (¼ gill, 3 cl) Cointreau
1 ounce (¼ gill, 3 cl) Lillet Blanc
1 ounce (¼ gill, 3 cl) fresh lemon juice
1 drop (not dash) of pastis (Pernod, Herbsaint, Ricard all will work,
  or use absinthe)

Shake in an iced cocktail shaker, and strain into cocktail glass. Drop a stemless
cherry into the bottom of glass.

The Corpse Reviver was more a class of drink than a single recipe. It originated
at the turn of the twentieth century, sometimes merely as the "reviver" or "eye
opener." At the time, however titled, it's meaning, was obvious: "hair of the dog" or
a little more of what bit you last night. As you may remember, this was the very way

the cocktail itself got its start 100 years before. One Corpse Reviver recipe was entered by name in a little British tome entitled *Drinks of All Kinds* in 1895, and by Prohibition there were perhaps four or five examples of them. Of my favorite, the #2, Savoy barman Harry Craddock cautioned, "Four taken in swift succession will unrevive the corpse again." Personally, I can't imagine drinking these in the morning, but then, no one has offered either.

Corpse Revivers are largely forgotten because, for a time, fruit juiced, complex, "up" cocktails went out of style. Drinking in the morning remained off limits to most people. The "Reviver" name was bound to Prohibition, and with the temporary ascendancy of highballs in the 1940s and beyond, it simply died out with the generation that drank such drinks.

You'll still have to track down at least one uncommon ingredient to make a Corpse Reviver #2: Lillet. Like Dubonnet, it has two varieties, red and white. One always chooses red Dubonnet, conversely, always choose Lillet Blanc. Like Dubonnet, Lillet is a delicate aperitif wine, and more specifically it is a quinquina—or quinine-containing aperitif—as are the two Dubonnets. No matter, unlike Dubonnet, you may have to search for Lillet or order it. With a little diligence, your search will be rewarded. . .it's not *that* uncommon.

DRINK NOTES

This is one of those cocktails that *must* be exactly measured to perform its magic. Here is a drink that, more than any other, shows just what delicate chemists these golden era bartenders often were. Not only is the drink beautiful to look at, every single ingredient shines through individually in each sip. The combination is harmonious; it's a slice of perfection.

Note, however, that most bars will not measure lemon juice, and they'll often try to sneak in sweet and sour mix instead. I've even seen them try to use Rose's Lime Juice Cordial. And even if they do use real lemon, they'll pull four or five wedges from the garnish tray and assume that's enough. They'll then free pour the alcohol and add a solid dash of the pastis. You'll end up with a sweet anise-tasting slurry. If you know a great bar with a serious bartender, bravo! For the rest of us, please. . . *do* try this at home first.

ABSINTHE: THE FINAL WORD

Since I mentioned it, I know you'll want to hear a little something about absinthe. Absinthe was banned in a number of countries some time between 1910 and 1915. The United States banned it in 1912.

Just as the temperance movement itself, chronicled in the history section of this book, was a knee-jerk reaction against the crime, indigence, family abandonment, and destitution burgeoning with increasingly urban and industrialized lifestyles, so was the ban on absinthe. In fact, one might say it was a dry run.

Absinthe is one minor constituent in classic cocktails, but one that receives an inordinate amount of fascinated attention. Here is the final word on absinthe: It is a bit bitter, it tastes like anise (sort of like licorice), it is very strong (though always served well diluted), and it remains banned largely on technicalities. As I've noted already: The thing withheld is the thing most desired. There came at the heels of cocktail resurgence an absinthe rebirth as well. You can get any number of brands and varieties of absinthe for a price via the Internet these days. My friend Ted Breau is soon to release several absinthes that exactly emulate the most famous pre-ban products. (I know of no one on Earth who knows more about absinthe than Ted.) If you want a bottle, just buy one. I've provided sources in the Resource Guide in the back of the book. When you've sampled a great number of them as I have, it becomes happily demystified and you realize it is just another ingredient and you either adore its character—or not.

The Modernista

❧

2 ounces (½ gill, 6 cl) Scotch
½ ounce (⅛ gill, 1.5 cl) dark Jamaican rum
1 teaspoon pastis (Pernod, Herbsaint, Ricard will all work, or use absinthe)
½ ounce (⅛ gill, 1.5 cl) Swedish Punsch
½ ounce (⅛ gill, 1.5 cl) fresh lemon juice
2 dashes orange bitters

Shake in an iced cocktail shaker, and strain into a cocktail glass. Add lemon twist.

❧

I must admit, this is *my* name for this drink, derived from the Modern Cocktail and sometimes called the Modern Maid. I thought the whole Scotch-pastis interaction showed promise, but the results were bitter. I readjusted the proportions and added the Swedish Punsch (which you can locate through the Resource Guide, page 137) to make a delightful, if challenging beverage.

Legendre orange bitters circa 1935; Carlshamn's Punsch circa 1970s (though the label had not changed one bit from the 1930s); Telephone, 1930s British General Electric; Cocktail shaker Forman Bros. circa 1936; *Just Cocktails* book dated 1939. Legendre Absinthe was only produced, as such, for 1 year; 1933. In 1934, the product became Herbsaint. Black & White Scotch dated 1939, "By appointment to His Majesty The King."

Vieux Carré Cocktail

1 ounce (¼ gill, 3 cl) rye whiskey
1 ounce (¼ gill, 3 cl) cognac
1 ounce (¼ gill, 3 cl) sweet vermouth
½ teaspoon Bénédictine
2 dashes Angostura bitters
2 dashes Peychaud bitters

Shake in an iced cocktail shaker, and strain onto fresh ice in a rocks glass.
Garnish with a lemon twist.

Tthe saddest forgotten cocktail is the one unknown where it was created. The
Vieux Carré (named for the old French term for New Orleans's French
Quarter—le Vieux Carré, "the Old Square") was invented by Walter Bergeron
sometime previous to the publication of
Stanley Clisby Arthur's *Famous New Orleans
Drinks and How to Mix Them* in 1937. Bergeron
was head bartender at what, 11 years later,
would become the Carousel bar in the
Monteleone Hotel. The drink's inclusion
here is courtesy of Chuck Taggart, devotee
of both classic cocktails and old New
Orleans. He tells of walking into the bar at
the Monteleone, ordering a Vieux Carré,
and receiving a nice refreshing glass of
"What's that?" for his trouble. Fortunately, it
seems with the cocktail resurgence that
orders for the Vieux Carré are once again up
at the bar there, and most bartenders at the
drink's birthplace can once again make it.

Circa 1934

DRINK NOTES

Recently, the Carousel Bar has taken to using dry vermouth in lieu of the sweet. It
works just fine that way, too.

Soyer au Champagne

In a parfait glass combine:

2 dashes maraschino liqueur
2 dashes pineapple juice
2 dashes orange Curaçao (or Grand Marnier)
2 dashes brandy

Fill glass with Champagne. Add a tablespoon of vanilla ice cream on top. Serve with a spoon and a straw.

Circa 1888. There are many recipes for this interesting beverage (which translates as "Silk with Champagne"), most containing ice cream. This is my favorite.

The Coffee Cocktail

1 ounce (¼ gill, 3 cl) brandy (Martell works well)
2 to 3 ounces (½ to ¾ gill, 6 to 9 cl) ruby port
1 egg
1 teaspoon sugar

Pour brandy into an iced cocktail shaker. Add the egg. Pour in the port and sugar.
Shake and strain into a small goblet. Grate or shake some nutmeg on top.

I remember with great fondness my first challenge to make Coffee Cocktails. I volunteered to produce some obscure drink—any obscure drink—for a little morning get-together at the Victorian home of Southern California historians Paul Greenstein and Dydia Delyser. Paul was quick with his vote, and this is but one of many clues to his comfortingly iconoclastic nature.

The Coffee Cocktail is entirely counterintuitive. For one thing, it contains no coffee. For another, unlike other cocktails contemporary to its creation, it contained no bitters. In other words, it was neither coffee nor cocktail. Even Jerry Thomas, who first published the recipe in the 1887 edition of his *Bar-Tender's Guide,* seemed uncharacteristically mystified.

> *The name of this drink is a misnomer, as coffee and bitters are not to be found among its ingredients, but it looks like coffee when it has been properly concocted, and hence probably its name.*

You'll note it *doesn't* look like coffee either. Ah, but in the morning after *real* coffee, it is counterintuitively delicious.

DRINK NOTES

The dreaded raw egg makes this a forgotten cocktail, but—as you will be told often in this book—be brave! See the Delicious Sour (page 52) for more information on this vital ingredient.

The Delicious Sour

2 ounces (½ gill, 6 cl) applejack
2 ounces (½ gill, 6 cl) peach-flavored brandy
Juice of 1 fresh lime (1 to 1½ ounces [(¼ to ⅓ gill, 3 to 4.5 cl])
1 egg white
1 teaspoon of sugar

Shake in an iced cocktail shaker, and strain into a goblet or large cocktail glass. Add a splash (about 1 ounce [¼ gill, 3 cl]) of soda water.

One of the better drinks from the 1892 book *The Flowing Bowl* by William "The Only William" Schmidt. Schmidt liked to be different. Many of the drinks in his book were unquestionably of his own creation. He liked to use ingredients no one else used, but this often resulted in drinks containing things like red wine and rum with a plop of vanilla ice cream. Here, and every now and again, he'd ring the bell and get a clear note.

DRINK NOTES

This is the second (but not the last) drink in this book to call for egg white as part of the recipe. *Raw* egg white. Truly, the Delicious Sour is an excellent example of how this occasionally maligned ingredient actually works in cocktails. It creates a border of soft foam. It gives the mouth-feel of each sip a soft silkiness. It embraces the other ingredients, unifying them. What it does *not* do is add flavor (like scrambled eggs were you thinking?). It also doesn't make the drink feel slimy. And last of all, it doesn't give you food poisoning. If you refrigerate your eggs, and if you bought them a week or less ago, you can bank on it. For the weak-kneed among you, the fact is, you can now buy pasteurized eggs, which eliminate *any* risk of diseases, such as salmonella, so you can now use raw eggs in drinks with impunity. Remember, though: The *main* reason egg white (and yolk) drinks are rarely made anymore is that they take a little extra time and effort to prepare, and they annoy the guy who washes the dishes.

If you are an egg-in-cocktail virgin, I have hints for you: Crack the egg just like you would if you were going to plop it into a pan, but once you've cracked it, move it immediately over the cocktail shaker. The white will *want* to come out. Balance the yolk in half of the egg shell. It'll be the same half from which the white is draining down into your shaker. Pour the yolk into the other half of the shell— which will encourage the rest of the white to separate and add itself into the shaker. Then toss out the shell and yolk, straighten your shoulders, and add the rest of the ingredients.

Hildick's apple brandy circa 1938; De Kuyper peach liqueur circa 1950

The Secret Cocktail

1 ½ ounces (⅓ gill, 4.5 cl) dry gin
½ ounce (⅛ gill, 1.5 cl) applejack
Juice of ½ lemon
1 egg white
2 dashes real pomegranate grenadine

Shake up with all due vigor in an iced cocktail shaker, strain into a cocktail glass, and serve with a cherry.

Just so you know, the real name of this drink is not the Secret Cocktail. I will, eventually, reveal its rightful title, but be forewarned, it has two characteristics that scare people to death: again, the dreaded egg and the drink name—it is enough to send virtually all men and most women running away, screaming.

This is a forgotten cocktail in the truest sense, but it is cloaked in familiarity because you can walk into virtually any bar and order one, if you have a mind to, but they will *all* be wrong, incorrect, not even close. ALL of them.

First concocted in the early twentieth century, The Clover Club Cocktail was named for the venerable Philadelphia men's club, created at the Bellevue-Stratford Hotel, and was consumed in copious quantities by its estimable members (financiers, attorneys, captains of industry, and traditional literary sorts). *Note:* The Secret Cocktail is not a Clover Club, but I must tell you what a Clover Club contained so you will understand the insanity surrounding the as-yet-unnamed cocktail of our discourse. It contained gin, lemon juice, an egg white, and a bit of grenadine. It was an opalescent, light-rose hue. Very fetching. Our Secret Cocktail contains the ingredients in the photograph shown here.

DRINK NOTES

Note the similarity to the Clover Club? Same production, same proportions. Men, however (and now most women), would not be caught dead ordering our little secret cocktail. . .the original Pink Lady. All the Pink Lady did was to add some applejack— which made the drink immeasurably tastier, but not one whit sweeter. It was also just a tad stronger, and the two cocktails were equally pink. Now you tell me. . .who was smarter, the guys or the dolls? Jury is in. The women win. So make this drink correctly for all your friends, but don't tell them the name of the drink until after they've tasted it.

Speas Apple Jack circa 1960; Gordon's gin circa 1940; Pinaud grenadine circa 1940; Crosby Gaige's *Cocktail Guide & Ladies' Companion*, 1945

Blood and Sand

1 ounce (¼ gill, 3 cl) Scotch
1 ounce (¼ gill, 3 cl) orange juice
¾ ounce (⅙ gill, 2 cl) cherry-flavored brandy
(Cherry Heering or Cherry Marnier are best.)
¾ ounce (⅙ gill, 2 cl) sweet vermouth

Shake in an iced cocktail shaker, and strain into a cocktail glass. Garnish with a cocktail cherry.

The Blood and Sand (named for the 1922 Rudolph Valentino movie) and the Vowel Cocktail, (page 125), are other perfectly tasty Scotch cocktails. You'll want to experiment with the Scotch you use, and I'll recommend starting with a good-yet-mild blend like Famous Grouse, a brand dear to my heart since that is just what Nurse Cocktail calls me.

DRINK NOTES

Scotch is a problematic cocktail ingredient. It has a reputation of not playing well with others. Really, there are only two mixed drinks made with Scotch that are *not* forgotten: The Rusty Nail (made with Scotch and Drambuie, a liqueur made from Scotch that tastes like Scotch) and the Rob Roy (a Manhattan with Scotch instead of rye or Bourbon).

Dewar's White Label Scotch circa 1922; Martini & Rossi vermouth circa 1946; Cusenier cherry liqueur circa 1940; cocktail shaker circa 1930s; Book, *Merton of the Movies*, published 1922

East India Cocktail

3 ounces (¾ gill, 9 cl) brandy
½ ounce (⅛ gill, 1.5 cl) raspberry syrup
1 dash Angostura bitters
1 teaspoon orange Curaçao
1 teaspoon maraschino liqueur

Shake in an iced cocktail shaker, and strain into a cocktail glass. Garnish with a cocktail cherry.

T his is another very, very old cocktail, and the recipe is one of many versions. The original, in Harry Johnson's *Bartender's Manual* of 1882, used pineapple syrup instead of raspberry, and some used both, but this is still a venerable variation, and I think preferable.

The Brooklyn Cocktail

⁂

2 ounces (½ gill, 6 cl) rye or Bourbon
¾ ounce (⅙ gill, 2 cl) dry vermouth
2 teaspoons Amer Picon
2 teaspoons maraschino liqueur

Stir in a mixing glass with ice, and strain into a cocktail glass. Garnish with a cocktail cherry.

⁂

Four of the five New York boroughs had cocktails of same name (pity poor Staten Island), but only the Manhattan achieved drink immortality. I want to remind you of two of the others. (Sorry, Queens.) You'll find the Bronx noted under the cuddly name the Income Tax Cocktail (page 68).

DRINK NOTES

Locate mixing rarities like Amer Picon and maraschino liqueur in the Resource Guide, page 137.

Vermouth circa 1940; Balsac maraschino liqueur circa 1946; J. W. Dant whiskey—distilled 1916 and bottled 1933; Amer Picon circa 1938; cocktail shaker circa 1930s

The French 75

2 ounces (½ gill, 6 cl) gin
1 ounce (¼ gill, 3 cl) lemon juice
2 teaspoon sugar or 1 teaspoon of simple syrup
Champagne

Shake all but the Champagne in an iced cocktail shaker. Pour into a tall glass (a collins glass, a zombie glass, or a Champagne flute will do—and I prefer the latter.) Fill with the Champagne. Stir gently, and garnish with a long, thin lemon spiral and a cocktail cherry.

Named after the French 75-mm field gun, model of 1897 (and companion shell). This bit of heavy artillery was *the* mainstay weapon of World War I, and its recoil system made for soft, smooth operation. It was really the first technical weaponry advance of the twentieth century, and its use continued into World War II.

The parallels between it and the cocktail named for it should be obvious. . .smooth, yet packs a wallop. Still, the drink itself is rather counterintuitive. Who would imagine combining gin and Champagne? Yet with the addition of a bit of sugar and a soupçon of fresh lemon juice, it is a refreshing delectation.

DRINK NOTES

One barman in 1947 called it a Tom Collins with Champagne instead of club soda. Vive la difference!

To be candid, this is a forgotten cocktail everywhere except New York City. There I have been able to walk into numerous bars and have the bartender whip one right up. The experience was akin to time travel, and I heartily recommend it.

If this drink has any problem, it is the misapprehension that it correctly contains brandy (Cognac) instead of gin. It is an error that has been infrequently repeated in various bar guides over time. As Robert "Drinkboy" Hess economically put it on his popular cocktail website, "Some people claim this drink should use Cognac instead of gin. Those people would be wrong." The Cognac version is properly designated the French 125. Named for another cannon? Of course not, why would you think that?

Angostura bitters circa 1945; Gilbey's gin dated 1937; Dom Perignon dated 1928

The Seelbach Cocktail

---

1 ounce (¼ gill, 3 cl) Bourbon (venerable Old Forester was specified)
½ ounce (⅛ gill, 1.5 cl) Cointreau
7 dashes Angostura bitters
7 dashes Peychaud bitters
5 ounces (1¼ gill, 15 cl) Champagne

Pour the Bourbon, Cointreau, and bitters into a Champagne flute, and stir. Add the Champagne. Stir again, and garnish with an orange twist.

The Seelbach was named for the Seelbach Hotel in Louisville, Kentucky, where it was born in 1917. That it can be published here is a testament to the diplomatic skills of cocktail scribes Gary and Mardee Regan.

The restaurant director for the hotel discovered the recipe (last served before Prohib-ition, and subsequently lost) in 1995. The director, Adam Seger, set about to produce it again, albeit with key ingredients kept secret. The Regans urged divulging the recipe, hinting at cocktail immortality in one of their fine drink books, and finally Seger submitted—requiring only that the formula be kept secret until the book's publication. That book, *New Classic Cocktails*, was published in 1997, and although the Seelbach Cocktail has been a matter of public record since then, I believe *Vintage Spirits & Forgotten Cocktails* is the second book to set it to print. After all, it's what this book is all about!

DRINK NOTES

The recipe, as supplied to the Regans, called for triple sec, not Cointreau. However, before Prohibition, the Cointreau bottle still read Cointreau Triple Sec. The liqueur was not only the *first* triple sec, it's how the term was coined. After imitators reproduced the signature square bottle and imprinted the words "Triple Sec" in the Cointreau typeface, Cointreau dropped the words from their bottle. The premium liqueur has long since transcended the category, but that's how it started out. . .the first and best triple sec. We therefore feel justified in calling for it here. Use generic triple sec only if you are short on cash.

Old Forester circa 1943; Peychaud bitters circa 1915; Cointreau dated 1936; Angostura bitters circa 1947; Veuve Cliquot Champagne vintage 1928—by many considered the finest Champagne vintage of the twentieth century; Picnic case circa 1920s

The Georgia Mint Julep

Muddle several fresh mint leaves in sugar and a dash of water in a silver julep cup.
   (A double-rocks glass works fine.)
Add 2 ounces (½ gill, 6 cl) Cognac (or other brandy), and
   1 ounce (¼ gill, 3 cl) peach-flavored brandy and crushed ice to fill.
Stir! Stir! Stir!
Insert several more fresh mint leaves between the cup and the mixture, sticking out
   and pointing heavenward.

1934 whiskey pamphlet

Here dwell no frowns, nor anger; from these gates
Sorrow flies far. See, here be all the pleasures
That fancy can beget on youthful thoughts,
When the fresh blood grows lively, and returns
Brisk as the April buds in primrose season.
And first behold this cordial julep here,
That flames and dances in his crystal bounds,
With spirits of balm and fragrant syrups mixed.
—John Milton, Comus (1634)

Peals of derisive laughter sound. The Mint Julep, a forgotten drink? Sir, have you
gone MAD? Every year they make 100s of gallons of the beverage at Churchill
Downs. Many a Southern bar muddles it with self-actualized flair. The Mint Julep
has been the subject of books, encyclopedia entries, and sonnets—so what balder-
dash is this!?

All of this is true, and of all the names for a drink, "julep" is by far the most ancient. Honestly, the Mint Julep has not been forgotten only once, but has waxed and waned several times since its origin. By the time mint was added (first notated after the conception but before the birth of the cocktail in 1803), it had already been forgotten at least for a time, but it was still more a name than a specific drink. When Kentucky Colonels sipped the minty fresh Bourbon sweetness of it, it had already retreated a second time, and it is of the earlier truly forgotten Mint Julep that I speak.

> The mint julep still lives, but it is by no means fashionable.
> Somehow the idea has gotten abroad that the mint ought to be
> crushed and shaken up with water and whiskey in equal propor-
> tions. No man can fall in love with such a mixture. Poor Juleps
> have ruined the reputation of the South's most famous drink.
>
> —*Bar-Tender's Guide, Jerry Thomas* (1887)

The Georgia Julep titled here is ironic in that the current Julep is most highly celebrated in Kentucky and the recipe for the one in this book is unquestionably from Northern Virginia! No matter, the Georgia prefix was assigned many years later and, assuredly, out of love. Though historians still argue over it, this Mint Julep, the first one for which a real recipe was printed, contained brandy—not whiskey. It's actually evident that mint, cracked ice, sugar, and any spirit on hand (generally rum, bourbon, rye, or brandy) were used, but most early narratives pinpointed brandy as liquor of choice. The formula I supply here is a variation of the one supplied in Frederick Marryat's *A Diary in America* (1839).

DRINK NOTES

The original recipe called for equal portions of the liqueur and the brandy. It was *far* too sweet by modern standards, though you can adjust, of course, to taste. By the twentieth century, recipes for the *Georgia* Mint Julep would often call for apricot-flavored brandy in lieu of the peach variety.

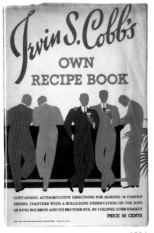

1934

This variation is just as good, if not better. Importantly, the mint should be spearmint. Irvin Cobb had this to say about it: "In the name of the julep I have seen high crimes and flagrant misdemeanors committed. . . .I have stood in horror and with seared eyeballs have seen a julep converted into a harsh green tea by the sacrilegious use of peppermint sprigs—not mint, peppermint! But if one's fancy inclines that way, why not just swallow a mothball and be done with it?"

Pink Gin

3 ounces (¾ gill, 9 cl) Plymouth Gin
6 goodly dashes Angostura bitters

Shake in an iced cocktail shaker. Strain into a stemmed cocktail glass, sans garnish.

Sounds cute doesn't it? Pink Gin—like sugar-coated barbed wire. Actually, it's worse than that. With the exception of raw egg, no two ingredients send green-horn drinkers galloping for the hills faster than gin and bitters. It only gets worse. Gin and bitters are the *only* ingredients in this cocktail. There is a trick, here—but first a bit of history and my own mea culpa.

The original Pink Gin was a favorite of the British Navy. This is the same navy that got a ration of Grog—rum and water. As was their wont, they drank these beverages warm (not warmed, just at cabin temperature). So, as for the Pink Gin, a couple dashes of Angostura bitters and a jigger of gin sufficed, presumably in a tin cup. Perhaps it's a good thing they deemphasized all that Naval boozing, but the drink still held promise.

Well, I changed the recipe—and I wasn't the only one. One thing I *didn't* change, though, was the type of gin they used. There are two brands of gin that work in this drink, all others fall *very* flat by comparison. It wasn't until recently that the brand always used by the sailors was available in the United States, after a long hiatus—Plymouth Gin—and it is miraculous stuff. It's velvety, but you see, even the company made changes. Back in the 1970s, they made it milder and lowered the proof. Spirits writer Tony Lord declared "Only two ex-Royal Navy men wrote to the company to complain." Since then, new owners have reissued the so-called Navy Strength version and produce it alongside the softer version. I love the smoothness of this gin. It is fortunate that through the tenacious efforts of the company, Plymouth is once again imported.

The only other brand that tastes right in a Pink Gin was Tanqueray Malacca—which adhered to an original 1839 gin formula, but in their infinite wisdom (heavy, HEAVY irony here) Tanqueray suspended its production. Plymouth and Malacca Gins are the most valued in Doc's liquor cabinet and I hope someone comes to their senses and produces the latter again.

As for our Pink Gin, we may continue to pursue its perfection. So here is what I did to make it acceptable to my oh-so American sensibilities: I tripled the amount of bitters. Six dashes is just fine. I used an iced cocktail shaker and insisted on the Plymouth Gin.

You're still shaking your head, I can see it from the other side of the book. Look, I can't explain it, but this particular gin when combined with the Angostura creates something more than the sum of its parts. It's amazing. I'll cajole you no longer, but think about this: I've gotten people who insisted they hate gin and hate bitters to *like* this drink. It's chemistry. Trust science.

Coates Plymouth Gin circa 1936; Angostura bitters circa 1900. Devices displayed are an assortment of hydrometers—alcohol percentage measurers—from the 1830s, the 1870s, and the 1930s. The electric razor is a Tarc from the 1930s. Ouch!

The Income Tax Cocktail

⚛

1½ ounces (⅓ gill, 4.5 cl) gin
¾ ounce (⅙ gill, 2 cl) dry vermouth
¾ ounce (⅙ gill, 2 cl) sweet vermouth
Juice of ¼ orange (squeezed right into the shaker)
2 dashes Angostura bitters

Shake in an iced cocktail shaker, and strain into a cocktail glass. Garnish with orange wheel.

⚛

It's name sends bolts of fear into otherwise staunch men! Writers and pundits disdained it! It could not live, and yet it wanted to live. It was the Bronx Cocktail to which the Income Tax merely added a couple dashes of Angostura bitters. In fact, if you wanted to feel particularly film noir, you'd lean over the dark bar you find yourself in and growl, "Bronx with bitters, and make it snappy!" Of course, since it is included in this book, you know they'd look at you like you just crawled out from under a rock, but really, what could be more film noir than that?

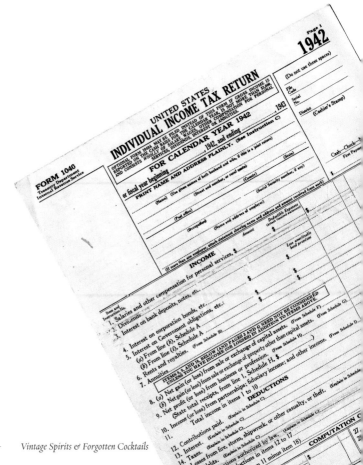

A master of the intoxicating phrase
BERNARD DeVOTO writes of
the cultural importance of hard liquor
and the only hour—the cocktail hour.

The Bronx, sister to the Manhattan, was a grand cocktail for many years. It fell prey to a chorus of Martini and highball voices rejecting the innocent orange juice it contained. In 1948, Bernard DeVoto, author of *The Hour* (on which the cover blurb reads ". . .the cultural importance of hard liquor and the only hour—the cocktail hour") called the Bronx the most ominous of a sore heritage of slops. Of course, he called the venerable Manhattan an "offence against piety" as well. The man was unyielding.

Mainly, the Bronx was easily ruined with packaged orange juice. It is a cocktail that *insists* on fresh-squeezed oranges, and for that reason alone it will not be made at many bars. The Income Tax is better still. The bitters add another dimension to the construction, and with correct measurements (not at all hard with this drink) and the fresh-squeezed juice, it is memorable and delicious.

DRINK NOTES

The superb architect Richard (Rick) Corsini introduced me to the "Bronx with bitters" as a Maurice. We both did a lot of vintage cocktail research using one another as guinea pigs, and the drink I would eventually identify, correctly, as the Income Tax was a real keeper. Many old bar guides refer to the drink as a Maurice, though it appears the true Maurice contained absinthe (or pastis) in lieu of bitters, taking it into Monkey Gland territory.

Mohawk Bronx Cocktail circa 1934; Italian vermouth circa 1930; Blackstone gin circa 1947; French vermouth circa 1940; Abbott's bitters circa 1912; cocktail shaker and glasses circa 1950s

Barnum (Was Right) Cocktail

2 ounces (½ gill, 6 cl) gin
1 ounce (¼ gill, 3 cl) apricot-flavored brandy (best is Marie Brizard's Apry)
2 dashes Angostura bitters
½ ounce (⅛ gill, 1.5 cl) fresh lemon juice

Shake in an iced cocktail shaker, and strain into a cocktail glass. Garnish with a lemon twist.

$\mathbf{I}$ngredient-wise, this appears to be a variation of the Pegu Club cocktail (page 96) and is superficially almost identical to the Barbara West. I must break it to you early in *Vintage Spirits & Forgotten Cocktails* that there are only a finite number of cocktail ingredients, and there are more now than there were when virtually all the drinks in this book were invented. Although this is a testament to the mixing prowess displayed by the pioneering parents of these libations, there is always the first inevitable letdown of the novice when he or she first mutters those glum words, "Hey! This is nothing but a Blah Blah Cocktail with a little Blah Blah Blah in it! Barnum *was right*...there's a fool born every minute!" Buck up. Once you try the many combinations, you'll happily see the devil (and the heart) in the nuances.

Mistletoe Gin circa 1933; Kord Apricot Liqueur circa 1940; cocktail shaker, Germany, circa 1930s; Elco Violet Ray machine (a quack medical device) circa 1930s; Book, *The Squire's Recipes*, dated 1912

This book purported to reproduce an eighteenth century recipe book which, if real, would've been the first cocktail reference. It was a notorious hoax. Note the "⅕ Gallon" statement on the Mistletoe bottle. Bottle sizes of the period were: ⅒ pint, ½ pint, 1 pint, 1 fifth, and a quart. That is what a fifth meant, ⅕ of a gallon, or ⅘ of a quart.

The Bebbo Cocktail

1½ ounces (⅓ gill, 4.5 cl) gin
1 ounce (¼ gill, 3 cl) fresh lemon juice
½ ounce (⅛ gill, 1.5 cl) honey
2 teaspoons orange juice

Stir all the ingredients (*except* the ice) together in a cocktail shaker until the honey dissolves. Add the ice, shake, and strain into a cocktail glass. Garnish with a cocktail cherry.

Another idiotically named drink, the Bebbo was based on the more desirably named Bee's Knees Cocktail, but with the addition of orange juice. The Bebbo has the last laugh. The Bebbo may have been forgotten, but it's here, whereas the Bee's Knees remains, justly, nowhere to be found.

DRINK NOTES

The secret trick with honey in cocktails is that, if possible, you should heat the honey to lessen its viscosity, thereby increasing its solubility. In layman's terms, it mixes better after heating.

The Filmograph Cocktail

2 ounces (½ gill, 6 cl) brandy
¾ ounce (⅙ gill, 2 cl) lemon syrup
(substitute fresh lemon juice unless you like to drink
maple syrup out of the can)
½ ounce (⅛ gill, 1.5 cl) kola tonic

Shake in an iced cocktail shaker, and strain into a cocktail glass. Garnish with a
lemon wedge.

This is a great cocktail name, redolent of old nitrate stock and silent-film stars. Unfortunately, the sweetness and the fact that 99 percent of the world has no idea what the hell "kola tonic" is, means that this drink has long been in the dust bin of cocktail history. I've remedied one problem by suggesting a juice instead of a syrup—and the other by directing you, dear reader, to a source for kola tonic—something akin to cola syrup. Back in the 1930s and before, they used to make an alcoholic version of kola tonic called, oddly, Tonicola. That may be gone, but thanks to the fact that kola tonic (made by Rose's of Lime Juice Cordial fame) is a staple of South African drinking, the cocktail can again be sipped.

1934 cocktail menu, Hotel Astor—New York City

The Aviation

2½ ounces (⅝ gill, 7.5 cl) gin
¾ ounce (⅙ gill, 2 cl) fresh lemon juice
2 or 3 dashes maraschino liqueur

Shake in an iced cocktail shaker, and strain into a cocktail glass. Garnish with a lemon twist.

The Aviation is well loved among classic cocktail habitués. It is simple, balanced, and pleasant tasting. Even William Grimes, *New York Times*'s critic of everyday life and author of the finest sociohistorical treatise on the cocktail yet written, thinks the Aviation rates high as an inappropriately forgotten cocktail. I like them, too, but they will forever be a bit spoiled for me because I have sipped Blue Moons.

A Blue Moon is exactly the same as an Aviation except the former calls for Crème Yvette, 30 years gone, and the latter uses maraschino liqueur. In most recipes, it is hard to beat the dry, natural flavor of maraschino liqueur. But Crème Yvette was a proprietary violet liqueur compounded from violet petals and other secret flavorings. Its generic counterpart was called crème de violette, still made in France by Benoit Serres under the name Liqueur de Violette. Made with Liqueur de Violette, the Blue Moon gives the Aviation a run for its money. Made with Crème Yvette (which was named for early twentieth century French actress Yvette Gilbert)—the Aviation doesn't stand a chance.

The Blue Moon has a delicate lace of light, semisweet floral flavor that dances with the snappy gin and the fresh, tart lemon. It is incomparable. Unfortunately, years ago, years after having bought the product from Sheffield (the originating company), Jacquin et Cie, still the owners of the formula and rights, saw fit to discontinue the liqueur. They also owned (and sadly altered and finally discontinued) Forbidden Fruit Liqueur. They haven't looked back. They developed products that sold better: Canton Ginger and, their star, Chambord, which comes in the same orb bottle Forbidden Fruit used to. All I can say is that it is too bad, because as good as the Aviation is, the Blue Moon was better. I hope Norton Cooper, savvy chairman of Jacquin et Cie will rethink this. Cocktails are back. The time for the reintroduction of these fine liqueurs is now.

Chatham Hotel Special

·:·:·

1½ ounces (⅓ gill, 4.5 cl) brandy
½ ounce (⅛ gill, 1.5 cl) ruby port
½ ounce (⅛ gill, 1.5 cl) cream
A dash of dark crème de cacao

Shake in an iced cocktail shaker, and strain into a small cocktail glass.

·:·:·

Circa midcentury, The Chatham, New York City. This is the only classic dessert cocktail I am including in the book. There are so many, and this one derives from several earlier, simpler ones—some, better known. The Chatham Special just seems to hit all notes just right. It is somehow restrained, perhaps even humble. In this way it makes the perfect delicious surprise.

Jacquin crème de cacao circa 1936; Gautier Cognac circa 1914; Ramos-Pinto Ruby Port, contemporary but with a label reproducing one of their 1920s posters. Gautier is alleged to be one of the Cognac houses bought out by Benedictine Fecamp in the 1930s to solely produce the brandy (the second "B") in the latter's new-but-wildly-popular B & B.

La Floridita Daiquiri

2 ounces ($^{1}\!/_{2}$ gill, 6 cl) rum (I like Havana Club, contraband from Cuba, or Brugal
    from the Dominican Republic)

Juice of $^{1}\!/_{2}$ lime (If your limes are small, use the whole thing)

1 teaspoon sugar or sugar syrup (Increase if too tart)

1 teaspoon maraschino liqueur

Blend with ice. Serve in a saucer cocktail or Champagne glass.

It is said the daiquiri was invented (in the sense that "necessity is the mother of invention") at the turn of the twentieth century by two copper mine engineers who used what was readily available all over Cuba—rum, limes, and cane sugar. *That* was an original Daiquiri. It was good, too. Even without the sugar, the lime had a perfect chemistry with the rum.

The La Florida Bar was the venue in Havana, Cuba, where Ernest Hemingway liked to drinks daiquiris, frozen. He only drank them there and only as made by the then–head bartender and eventual owner Constantino (Constante) Ribalaigua. Locals referred to the place as La Floridita, a diminutive form of the name, like calling a baby "babykins"—an assignment of affection.

Those are the facts, from there the story goes straight to hell. In dispute are the recipe and ingredients for La Floridita Daiquiri and whether it is the special Daiquiri Hemingway liked to drink. The seeds of fame were, as ever, harbingers of discord. In Charles Schumann's emblematic *Tropical Bar Book* (1989), La Floridita Daiquiri is plainly listed much as the one I recommend here, though not blended. It was to be mixed in a shaker and with crushed ice. He also lists a Florida Daiquiri, which halves the lime juice and adds grapefruit juice. He has been challenged on these recipes, though, and some sorting out is in order. The 1947 *Bartender's Guide* by *Trader Vic* (rum king in the minds of many) lists *four* La Florida Daiquiris (note the lack of the diminutive form), all of which contain *lemon* juice in lieu of the lime. This was simply a mistranslation owed to the original La Florida bar guide give-aways in the 1930s.

The Cuban word for "lime" is *limón*. Their word for "lemon" is also *limón*. The key is in the modifying word (or lack thereof) after limon. A lime is a *limón verde*, a lemon is a *limón*. The English translation of these guides didn't make the leap. They translated limon verde as *lemon* and Trader Vic Bergeron merely repeated the translated form—and the mistake. He also listed a Trader Vic's Daiquiri, which was the Schumann recipe, albeit with Puerto Rican rum and blended. By his 1972 revised edition, he had corrected the lemon/lime mistake, but also confused the situation further, listing no La Florida Daiquiris at all, but including one La Floridita Daiquiri, blended—with the recipe that used the grapefruit juice. To roil the waters even further, he included a La Florida *Cocktail* (with crème de cacao) as well. In the 1934 *Bar La Florída Bar Cocktails* guide, composed while Constante

was a bartender working for then-owner Segundo Menendez, all daiquiris appear by number. Schumann's La Floridita is Daiquiri #4, tellingly subtitled (Florida Style) served with crushed ice from an "electric shaker." This guide also includes [groan] a Floridita Special that contains no rum at all. By their 1939 edition, Constante owned the bar. He listed five daiquiris, all shaken, #3 the grapefruit variety, #4 the one we suggest here, both shaken.

Bacardi gold rum—Cuba circa 1936. Bacardi white rum—Cuba circa 1959 (some of the last to be bottled before Castro commandeered the distillery.) Havana Club circa 1939—when the Arechabala family was still at the helm. Coco Rumbas cookie tin circa 1940s, Balzac maraschino liqueur circa 1946. Hamilton Beach Ron Rico Daiquiri Mixer circa 1948.

The #4 is now subtitled (Howard & Mac). The lime/lemon translation mistake continues, but we all know what was meant. . .lime. Two pages beyond the daiquiri recipes is listed a cocktail entitled the "E. Henminway [sic] Special." It was the grapefruit recipe, blended.

Sometime between 1934 when he worked there and 1939 when he owned the place, Constante Ribalaigua created this drink not yet termed "a daiquiri" for Ernest Hemingway. Was it the one Hemingway liked to drink? We don't know, but it was named after him and it was frozen; we can suppose it was.

It doesn't matter one whit what Papa Hemingway drank. In simplicity is profundity. Here is the recipe I believe to be the pinnacle of the classic daiquiri art—and I'll wager Hemingway drank them before Constante mixed his first "Henminway Special."

Published here is the exact lost recipe from the 1934 *Bar La Florida Cocktails* guide. Double quantities for a larger cocktail. These days, almost any drink made with rum is a "daiquiri." Suffice to say, the formula I give—and *all* the recipes referenced under this heading—are wholly different animals.

1928

The Widow's Kiss

1½ ounces (⅓ gill, 4.5 cl) Calvados
¾ ounce (⅙ gill, 2 cl) Chartreuse
   (Green was meant, but yellow mellows the drink a bit)
¾ ounce (⅙ gill, 2 cl) Bénédictine
2 dashes Angostura bitters

Shake in an iced cocktail shaker, and strain into a cocktail glass. Garnish with a cherry run through on a ruby hat pin. (Oops! The metaphor is running away with me—just a cherry will do.)

As the scene opens, you are up in your grandmother's attic opening the dusty steamer trunk she brought from Europe in 1914. You reverently turn back layer upon layer of old lace and brocade...unveiling a packet of old love letters tied in silk ribbon. Ancient dried rose petals flutter down from between the envelopes.

That is what the Widow's Kiss is like. Sweet, complex, and darkly golden; thought provoking and introspective. It is a cocktail of fall turning toward winter, and it wins Doc's award as the most evocative drink ever. Have one by the fire.

DRINK NOTES

Harry Johnson, the perpetual underdog (he authored the *second* important cocktail guide ever, to his never-ending chagrin) appears to have actually been the second again to print up a Widow's Kiss recipe in the 1900 edition of his *Bartender's Manual*. Oh well, some guys never get a break. The first publication seems to have been in the book *Modern American Drinks*, written by George Kappeler in 1895.

Now as much as I adore applejack, the Widow's Kiss is one drink where I must insist on Calvados. Not only is it in keeping with the classy character of the drink— as defined by its name—but even cheap Calvados works wonders preserving the ultra-smooth, brooding nuance of this superb cocktail.

So what happened to the Widow's Kiss? No single decisive event turned this cocktail into a forgotten one, but various trends conspired over time to do so. By the time the Savoy's Harry Craddock republished the recipe in 1930, people were moving away from herbal liqueurs like Chartreuse and Bénédictine.

Benedictine dated 1936; Hildick's Applejack circa 1960; Liqueur Jaune (a Chartreuse imitation) circa 1934; Angostura bitters circa 1940s. Also shown are an assortment of 1930s and 1940s linen cocktail napkins and a dancing trophy which, like the Liqueur Jaune, was a knockoff; in this case of Chicago's Aragon Ballroom, this pretender in California. The trunk belonged to my grandmother, and held her belongings for her trip from England to Virginia in 1914.

The 110-proof green version of Chartreuse dates back to 1605. The young upstart yellow version only appeared in 1838. Bénédictine's recipe was even earlier (1510) but was not commercially produced until 1863. Originally, both liqueurs were made by monks, and Chartreuse still is. As with gin (and before that alcohol itself), these

herbal potions were considered medicinal. By the cocktail era, though, they were unquestionably recreational. The point is, in the centuries before ready refrigeration, herbal liqueurs kept. I've opened 100-year-old bottles of Chartreuse and Bénédictine and found them (at least) as good today as when they were produced. This is not the case with fruit liqueurs. We now live in a heyday of natural-tasting fruit flavors, but there was a time when getting these flavors into alcohol—and getting them to *stay* in alcohol—was next to impossible. Even now, a very old bottle of orange liqueur is liable to taste more like molasses than orange.

Eventually distillation, flavoring, and preservation techniques were stabilized and perfected and fruit liqueurs became *very* popular. Herbal liqueurs, with heady flavors—some associated with medicinal preparations—took a back seat. By 1930, this was certainly so. In the twenty-first century, it is the rare imbiber who has any idea how to appreciate the potent, complex, aromatic flavors of herbal liqueurs. But the Widow's Kiss makes that effort truly worthwhile.

Calvados also remains uncommon in America. It can be found but you'll have to search. Most Calvados is well aged and it is all made in France. It can be expensive. (About once a year, Trader Joe's Company, a grocer, gets in a shipment of minimally aged Calvados for about 10 bucks a bottle. Being Dr. Cocktail, I stock up. You may not be able to find bargains like that, but a single bottle once a year remains a fine cocktail investment at well above that price.) A recent Web search located $15 bottles. Chartreuse can be more than $40 a bottle, but it keeps well nigh forever, and a little goes a long way.

The Derby Cocktail

---

1 ounce (¼ gill, 3 cl) Bourbon
½ ounce (⅛ gill, 1.5 cl) sweet vermouth
½ ounce (⅛ gill, 1.5 cl) orange Curaçao
¾ ounce (⅙ gill, 2 cl) fresh lime juice
Add mint leaf

Shake in an iced cocktail shaker, and strain into a cocktail glass.

There has always been a certain simpatico correspondence between the cocktail and The Races. The Mint Julep has become a mascot, of sorts, for its race (the Kentucky Derby) but, as with the Futurity or the Derby here, cocktails were actually named to commemorate races as well. The Derby had several variations. Three were listed in the 1947 Bar Guide by Trader Vic, and this is my favorite of those.

The Millionaire Cocktail

1½ ounces (⅓ gill, 4.5 cl) Myers's Original Dark Rum
¾ ounce (⅙ gill, 2 cl) sloe gin
¾ ounce (⅙ gill, 2 cl) apricot brandy
Juice of 1 fresh lime (1 to 1½ ounces [¼ to ⅓ gill, 3 to 4.5 cl])

Shake as though with the heeby jeebies in an iced cocktail shaker. Strain into a cocktail glass. Garnish with a lime wedge.

Bartenders and drink writers have a dirty little cocktail secret. Recipes are not sacred. You can *change* a drink if it doesn't suit you. Oh, I wouldn't try it with any of the drinks in MY book. . .they are *perfect*. All others, though, are a matter of drinkers' tastes. That is why there are so many close variations of classic and modern cocktails. Every bartender and every patron wants their drinks made in the manner that best suits them.

So here we have the Millionaire. I found the recipe for it in *The How and When* of 1937. It was actually the Millionaire #4 as written up in that book, and Millionaire #1 in 1930's *Savoy Cocktail Book*. (Numbers like that were once a time-honored way to catalog drink variations and entirely different drinks that happened to have the same name.) I have been guilty of calling out "Millionaire #4," and I suppose among those familiar with the book it might help to pinpoint exactly what drink is being discussed, but it really isn't right. Unless you can specify a temporal order to such numbered drinks, they all deserve to be number one. In truth, they are all simply "Millionaires." In other cases, and certainly since the cocktail revival, drink variations get their own names, such as the Martini becomes a Gibson merely by changing the garnish from a twist or olive to a cocktail onion.

The 1937 recipe for the Millionaire #4 was as follows:
Juice of 1 lime, 1 dash grenadine, ⅓ part sloe gin, ⅓ part apricot brandy, ⅓ part Jamaica rum.

Who sees the problems? To begin with, that recipe serves up a sickeningly sweet drink. Apricot brandy isn't a brandy—it is a brandy-based liqueur. That poor little lime doesn't stand a chance. Also, quality sloe gin is wonderful stuff, but besides being sweet, it is also very potent. The poor rum doesn't stand a chance. Finally, what the hell is that dash of sweet grenadine syrup doing in there at all, considering Sloe gin is every bit as red as grenadine?

So (rolling up my sleeves) here is the Doctor's remedy:

1) Double the rum, and use Myers's (the strongest-flavored Jamaican rum on the market),

2) Use the exact proportions in the recipe, which gives the lime an edge.

3) Delete the grenadine.

Gordon's Sloe Gin circa 1939; both bottles of Myers's Plantation Punch rum with stated age of 8 years—circa 1936; Apricot liqueur circa 1888; Biscuit (cookie) tin circa 1935; Figurine (actually a decanter) circa 1940

DRINK NOTES

This incarnation has a nice balance between sweet and tart and strong. It has the character of a tropical cocktail with unexpected flavors. Quality ingredients really help this drink out. Besides the aforementioned Myers's, I recommend Marie Brizard Apry as your apricot-flavored brandy and the domestic Mohawk as a good sloe gin. The very best is Plymouth Sloe Gin from England, but they have not seen fit to import it as of yet. Again, I have seen bartenders ruin this cocktail by not measuring or by shaking like they are afraid it's nitroglycerin. You want it cold and you want it tart enough to balance the rich flavors. Once a bartender learns to make it correctly, you too can experience the thrill of commanding, "Bartender, make me a Millionaire!"

Knickerbocker à la Monsieur

2 ounces ($^1\!/_2$ gill, 6 cl) Virgin Islands rum
$^1\!/_2$ ounce ($^1\!/_8$ gill, 1.5 cl) orange Curaçao
$^1\!/_2$ ounce ($^1\!/_8$ gill, 1.5 cl) raspberry syrup
1 ounce ($^1\!/_4$ gill, 3 cl) lemon juice
1 slice of orange
1 slice of pineapple

Add all to crushed ice in a goblet, collins glass, or tumbler, stir, and serve. Garnish with more fruits in season.

This nineteenth century hit had "his" and "hers" versions—à la Monsieur and à la Madame. Both were published in 1869 in William Terrington's *Cooling Cups and Dainty Drinks*. In 1888, Harry Johnson printed the manly version shown here.

The Monkey Gland

1½ ounces (⅓ gill, 4.5 cl) dry gin

1½ ounces (⅓ gill, 4.5 cl) orange juice (fresh squeezed makes it unimaginably good)

1 teaspoon real pomegranate grenadine

1 teaspoon pastis plus 1 dash of pastis (Pernod, Herbsaint, Ricard will all work, or
    use absinthe—which can be ordered from Europe. See Resource Guide, page 137.)

Shake vigorously in an iced cocktail shaker, and strain into a small cocktail glass.

Prohibition turned out to be a boon to rebellious cocktail creation. The symbolic flagship of the Prohibition venue was undoubtedly Harry's Bar, which was far from American shores: I do not mean the famous one named after Harry Pickering in Venice, Italy, cozy and traditional as it might be. . .but rather the 1920s beehive of activity that was Harry McElhone's joint, Harry's New York Bar—situated, ironically, in Paris. This 1920s beehive of activity embodied the spirit of Gatsby, of flappers, and of moneyed Americans abroad. From this wellspring flowed the cocktail that, to my mind, is most associated with Prohibition, the Monkey Gland.

I always felt like eighty-three
Standing 'round like an old oak tree
But something wonderful happened to me;
Just wait and see.
A little operation
Filled me full of syncopation
And now I shout with glee!
(monkey screech) I'm just a monkey man.
I feel like a wild monkey
Looking for a chimpanzee.
(monkey screech) See this monkey talk.
Every day in every way I'm getting better in my monkey walk.
(monkey screech) I'm wild as wild can be.
(monkey screech) So don't you monkey with me.
Since my recovery, the other day
I made a discovery, and that's why I say
Understand
It was a monkey gland
That made a monkey out of me.

"Made a Monkey Out of Me" Meyers,
Black, & Schoebel 1923, Original
Memphis Melody Boys featuring Billy
Meyers, the Original Monkey Man

Veteran vaudevillian Billy Myers sang of it in "Made a Monkey Out of Me," whose lyrics contain an extended double entendre: referring to how the drink presumably made you act and the procedure from which its name derived. This medical procedure, pioneered by Dr. Serge Voronoff and very au courant in Paris in the midtwenties, involved transplanting a monkey testicle into male humans to "rejuvenate" them. Claims were made of it being a veritable fountain of youth, but it was really the promise of the gland's aphrodisiac effects that caught everyone's imagination.

DRINK NOTES

Some recipes substitute Bénédictine for the risky absinthe or its substitutes. It was once a bit of a trend, and was done to several old absinthe-containing cocktails. Whereas learned cocktailians Gary and Mardee Regan prefer this style, I find the original recipe remains entirely persuasive and is, in fact, a crowd pleaser. Some also vary it by using 2 ounces (½ gill, 6 cl) gin to 1 ounce (¼ gill, 3 cl) orange juice.

Pa-Poose grenadine, New Orleans circa 1950s; Pernod absinthe circa 1910; Booth's gin circa 1933; *Prohibition at its Worst*, 1926; *The Saloon in the Home*, 1930

The latter book made righteous fun of the Noble Experiment, pairing fervent temperance songs with cocktail recipes.

The Scoff Law Cocktail

1½ ounces (⅓ gill, 4.5 cl) rye
1 ounce (¼ gill, 3 cl) dry vermouth
¾ ounce (⅙ gill, 2 cl) fresh lemon juice
¾ ounce (⅙ gill, 2 cl) real pomegranate grenadine

Shake in an iced cocktail shaker, and strain into a cocktail glass. Garnish with a lemon twist.

1930

Another entry in the Prohibition drinks market, the Scoff Law *drink* followed the coining of the actual term (in 1924) by less than two weeks. Another invention of Harry's New York Bar in Paris, the cocktail hilariously baited Prohibition sensibilities (the term originally referred specifically to a frequenter of speakeasies and general flouter of the National Prohibition Act). The Scoff Law Cocktail was barman Jock's bibulous answer to the vocabulary of castigation.

DRINK NOTES

Some recipes erroneously call for Canadian whisky instead of rye, probably because blended Canadian whisky often contained a higher percentage of rye to, say, *uranium.* (For those of you who aren't whiskey aficionados *yet*, most blended "whiskey" contains about 87 percent grain neutral spirits—basically grain alcohol— to 13 percent whiskey, which is divided into corn and rye or wheat components. Therefore, calling a Canadian blend "rye" because it contains more rye probably means it contains, say, 8 percent rye instead of 5 percent—not very compelling!) With good ryes once again on the market, using a blend is particularly misguided.

There is also an oft-published variation of the Scoff Law substituting Chartreuse for grenadine. I like Chartreuse, but avoid this variation at all costs unless you need an emetic.

The Blackthorn Cocktail

2 ounces (½ gill, 6 cl) gin
¾ ounce (⅙ gill, 2 cl) Red Dubonnet
¾ ounce (⅙ gill, 2 cl) kirschwasser

Stir in a mixing glass with ice, and strain into a cocktail glass. Garnish with a cocktail cherry and a lemon twist.

There were many renditions of the Blackthorn Cocktail, stretching well back into the nineteenth century. This one, of more recent origin, was the most singular.

The Blinker Cocktail

2 ounces ($^1\!/_2$ gill, 6 cl) rye
1 ounce ($^1\!/_4$ gill, 3 cl) grapefruit juice
1 teaspoon or 2 bar spoons raspberry syrup

Shake in an iced cocktail shaker, and strain into a cocktail glass. Garnish with a lemon twist.

DRINK NOTES

Grenadine was specified in the original recipe from Patrick Gavin Duffy's *Official Mixers Manual* (1934). I was experimenting with substitutions for it that were used in the nineteenth century and in Europe. I tasted the Blinker with raspberry syrup—woefully underused in cocktails—and never looked back.

Palm Beach Special

2½ ounces gin (I like Bombay Sapphire in this one.)
¾ ounce (⅙ gill, 2 cl) grapefruit juice
½ ounce (⅛ gill, 1.5 cl) sweet vermouth

Shake in an iced cocktail shaker, and strain into a cocktail glass.

A product of the 1940s, the Palm Beach could hardly be simpler, but it is also crisp, bracing, and effective. . .like a New Yorker. I believe in the naming, though, it and the next cocktail were switched at birth.

Park Avenue Cocktail

2 ounces (½ gill, 6 cl) gin
¾ ounce (⅙ gill, 2 cl) pineapple juice
¾ ounce (⅙ gill, 2 cl) sweet vermouth
2 teaspoons orange Curaçao

Shake in an iced cocktail shaker, and strain into a cocktail glass.

Like the Palm Beach at left, a 1940s cocktail of easy mixing. Note the tropical character, invoking Carmen Miranda strutting down a New York boulevard. As I say, the names of these two cocktails were obviously switched at birth!

1935

Pegu Club Cocktail

1½ ounces (⅓ gill, 4.5 cl) gin
½ ounce (⅛ gill, 1.5 cl) Cointreau
¾ ounce (⅙ gill, 2 cl) fresh lime juice
2 dashes Angostura bitters

Shake in an iced cocktail shaker, and strain into a cocktail glass.

Here out West in the broad lands of the sun and the stars, everyone drives, and drinking is done with some caution. The classic cocktail lifestyle is often merely an affectation in the Hollywood environs and for good reason. Walking cities like New York, San Francisco, and London can practice moderation yet still partake in a few small cocktails, like sampling tapas, before the stroll home. In Los Angeles,

therefore, there are precious few career bartenders and those that remain are nearing retirement. With the maturation of the cocktail revival, even out here we've begun to hear voices of reason calling for smaller, fresher, better cocktails consumed with restraint and forethought. No voice is clearer or more persuasive in this clarion call than that of Daniel Reichert, the man behind vintagecocktails.com. When asked what his favorite forgotten cocktail was, he paused in reflection. There are, after all, so many.

1934

There *was* the Pegu Club, though. A 1920s product of British colonial Burma, christened and served in the club of the same name. The Pegu was his choice.

DRINK NOTES

Reichert's enthusiasm for the drink bound me to use his preferred recipe. Most I've seen call for orange Curaçao instead of Cointreau and include a dash of orange bitters along with the Angostura. No matter, half cocktail and half dream, it is excellent prepared either way.

Circa 1935

Picon Punch

Fill a collins or highball glass with ice.
Add 1 teaspoon real pomegranate grenadine and 2½ ounces (⅝ gill, 7.5 cl) Amer Picon (Torani Amer).
Fill with soda water.
Float 1 ounce (¼ gill, 3 cl) brandy on top.
Très délicieux.

This is the grandest of Basque drinks and though in the past it has been associated with San Francisco, in no place are more Picon Punches consumed per capita, than in Bakersfield, California—home of several Basque restaurants and even more bars. Bakersfield is a wonderful place if you're there for the Basque traditions (and the Picon Punch) and not the scenery (of which it has little). Mainly, they made wonderful Picon Punch—which is itself a miracle. There were many renditions of the Blackthorn Cocktail, stretching well back into the nineteenth century. This one, of more recent origin, was the most singularhe House of Picon has had its problems, at least with distribution in the States, but extending back further in France to when,

Prohibition era

inexplicably, they changed the proof (and certainly the flavor) of Amer Picon from about 35 percent to about 12 percent alcohol. Fortunately, though I feel so wrong saying so, there is a better, though more obscure product on the market. It matches the Amer Picon proof from days of yore, and its flavor is more in keeping with traditional Picon Punch. This product, Torani Amer, is made in the United States, and every bar in Bakersfield stocks it. Talk about a testimonial. Picon Punch may be obscure, but it's not the only tipple in the book calling for Amer Picon—ahem—I mean Torani Amer. Still, I hope Picon straightens out distribution and formula. It would otherwise foretell the sad end to a historic product.

Trader Vic grenadine dated 1947, considered by some to be the finest grenadine ever made; White Rock mineral water circa 1947, from the cellar of Cecil B. DeMille. Amer Picon circa 1960; Hennessy Cognac circa 1947; portable Orthophonic Victrola circa 1939

DRINK NOTES

Note: If the brand Torani sounds familiar, and your mind wanders to coffee flavoring syrups. . .you'd be right. You'll never find their Amer anywhere *near* their other products, though. It alone contains alcohol.

The Calvados Cocktail

1½ ounce (¼ gill, 3 cl) Calvados
1½ ounce (¼ gill, 3 cl) orange juice
¾ ounce (⅙ gill, 2 cl) Cointreau
¾ ounce (⅙ gill, 2 cl) orange bitters

Shake in an iced cocktail shaker, and strain into a cocktail glass. Add an orange wheel to garnish.

Isn't it interesting that society movies were popular in the depths of the Depression? People struggling for every dime didn't resent photoplays of the elite in dramas or comedies. For the short hours in the theaters, *they* were the beau monde, eager to trade in their own lives for the fantasy. So it was with cocktails; a departure from the overcast and humdrum into the delicate, colorful, and bright.

Two cocktails that illustrate this perfectly are the entirely Unforgotten Champagne Cocktail—a drink that has not changed one iota in 140 years—and the Calvados Cocktail.

As far as I am able to determine, the Calvados Cocktail first saw print in Harry Craddock's beautifully designed *Savoy Cocktail Book*, published in London in 1930. This book also saw a simultaneous printing in the United States, which was a rather frisky move considering Prohibition's repeal was still three years off. Ah, but the writing was already on the wall. The public no longer could stomach Prohibition, and in the shadow of the Great Depression, its fate was sealed.

1932 vehicle bumper plate

DRINK NOTES

Now at first blush, this drink sounds like a condensation of the Golden Dawn (page 38). The reason it isn't is the massive jolt of orange bitters it calls for. In fact, depending on the brand of orange bitters you choose, you may just want to pull back a little on the quantity you add. Even so, this cocktail is more like an Orange Negroni than the Golden Dawn.

Calvados, for the uninitiated, is a special apple brandy from France. The scarcity of orange bitters, however, is the chief reason this is a forgotten cocktail. The story of how orange bitters were rediscovered to the benefit of the cocktail revival is a great one. You can read about it, and all things orange bitters, under the Satan's Whiskers recipe (page 106).

American apple brandy—distilled 1913 and bottled 1919; Palais Royale orange bitters circa 1934; Cointreau (note the term "triple sec" still appears on the label) circa 1913; *Savoy Cocktail Book* dated 1930

Pendennis Cocktail

⁂

2 ounces (½ gill, 6 cl) gin
1 ounce (¼ gill, 3 cl) apricot (some say peach) brandy
2 or 3 dashes Peychaud bitters
¾ ounce (⅙ gill, 2 cl) fresh lime juice (½ lime)

Shake in an iced cocktail shaker, and strain into a cocktail glass.

⁂

There have been many variations of the cocktail, named for the private club in Louisville, Kentucky, famously (but erroneously) also credited for the invention of the Old-Fashioned (page 134). This one is enticing.

Mohawk apricot liqueur skyscraper bottle circa 1934; Baldwin Brothers gin dated 1919; Figurine decanter circa 1934, cocktail biscuit tin circa 1940

Ritz Sidecar

5 parts old Cognac
3 parts Cointreau
2 parts fresh lemon juice

Shake in an iced cocktail shaker, strain tremulously into a chilled cocktail glass, and
stare at the treasure in rapt silence for a full 15 seconds before quaffing.
(Frank's original turn on the recipe was 2 parts old Cognac, 1 part each Cointreau
and lemon juice.)

Colin Field champions this rarified version of the Sidecar Cocktail. Mr. Field is
head bartender and inheritor of the mantle of Frank Meier, barmaster of the
Ritz Bar in Paris during the golden age of cocktails. The amicable Colin offers up a
cocktail experience possibly requiring a lavish trip to Paris:

"The difficulty in producing that one today is that the Ritz Sidecar is made with pre-phylloxera Cognac. In fact, it's even more astute to use pre-odium 1854. That was when trouble started here in France, massive national scale trouble, and phylloxera vastatrix just finished us off totally."

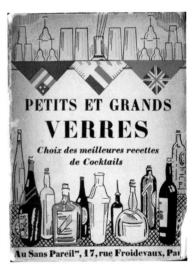

1930

[*Doc's note:* Odium was a mildew like fungus that decimated French vineyards. Phylloxera were plant lice that utterly devastated French—and global—grape vines in the early 1860s. It is said that wine and cognac produced before the destruction were better than any since.]

"All that to say that we still do the cocktail. It is in the *Guinness Book of World Records* as the most expensive cocktail in the world and at the moment I'm using an 1853 E. Remy Martin Cognac to do the Sidecar. A bottle that has been in the hotel since 1898, although the Germans nearly put their hands on it! Sometimes I use 1834 or even 1813. Although 99.99 percent is sold just as Cognac of course. As the holder of the keys of Ritz head bartender tradition, I'm just doing the best I can so that Frank's Cocktail lives on as long as possible. It's 400 Euros at the moment. . ."

When I said to Colin, I'd love one, he replied, "Frankly, so would I." (For a sidecar
you *can* make, see the Great Old Standards section in this book.)

Doctor Cocktail

2 ounces (½ gill, 6 cl) Jamaica rum
1 ounce (¼ gill, 3 cl) Swedish Punsch
1 ounce (¼ gill, 3 cl) fresh lime juice

Shake in an iced cocktail shaker, and strain into a cocktail glass. Garnish with a lime twist.

Another *Trader Vic* variation—though similar to the one promoted in 1936 by Frank Meier of the Ritz Bar in Paris—this time of my namesake drink. Most Doctor Cocktail recipes were closer to the Have a Heart Cocktail (page 120) sans grenadine, but Frank Meier and Victor Bergeron were right. Swedish Punsch is a rum-based, rum-flavored liqueur. Combining it with rum and rum's little buddy the lime was a no-brainer.

Myers's 1879 distilled 1942 and bottled 1954; Seltzer siphon circa 1930s; electric cocktail mixer—1933

Satan's Whiskers Cocktail

(Curled)
½ ounce (⅛ gill, 1.5 cl) gin
½ ounce (⅛ gill, 1.5 cl) dry vermouth
½ ounce (⅛ gill, 1.5 cl) sweet vermouth
½ ounce (⅛ gill, 1.5 cl) orange juice
2 teaspoons orange Curaçao
1 teaspoon orange bitters

Shake in an iced cocktail shaker, and strain into a cocktail glass. Garnish with an orange twist.

The straight version uses Grand Marnier instead of Curaçao.

Not all classic cocktails have great names to go with their formulas, but one could hardly do better than Satan's Whiskers. There are two varieties—*curled*, when mixed one way, or *straight*, when mixed another. This cocktail first appeared in Harry Craddock's *Savoy Cocktail Book* in 1930. I could hardly put it better than *HotWired* did when they said:

> We contend that the 'curled' Satan's Whiskers is more diabolic. . . We sip our
> Satan's Whiskers curled if it's still light outside and straight if it's not.

I've polled the experts, and while the majority prefer it straight, I must side with *HotWired* on this one. Besides, from first publication they were always listed together, so the choice has remained ours to make.

DRINK NOTES

Perhaps one of the reasons people prefer the straight variety is that they've never had really good Curaçao. Marie Brizard makes one, but it tastes to me more like Grand Marnier than a classic Curaçao. Top-notch Bardinet Orange Curaçao can be ordered from Europe, and it isn't expensive. I'll divulge my sources in the back of the book. What makes both varieties of Satan's Whiskers forgotten cocktails, though, are the orange bitters, which though uncommon, can be found or ordered.

ORANGE BITTERS

Orange bitters all but dropped out of sight in the 1960s when Schiefflin stopped producing Old House Orange Bitters, a sad demise for a wonderful brand. The story of how orange bitters again found their way into current-day cocktails is connected inextricably to this drink, too.

In 1992, to the exclusion of all else, I was researching classic cocktails, acquiring vintage bar guides and the booze to concoct the drinks they enumerated. The most frustrating aspect was the shear number of delicious-sounding recipes that called for orange bitters. I couldn't find those bitters anywhere. No one carried them and I was beginning to think they were extinct.

I was flipping through my newly acquired copy of Phillip Collins's marvelous piece of eye candy, *The Art of the Cocktail*, when I noticed with wide eyes he had a recipe for a Satan's Whiskers included, and it contained orange bitters. I had just gotten the book and it was brand new. Not only did it contain the recipe, but a *photo* of the drink as well! Obviously Collins and his bartender Ryan Sage knew where to get orange bitters, otherwise how could they have made the drink in the picture? I was a man on a mission. I called Mr. Collins's publisher and asked where he obtained his orange bitters. They would get back to me as soon as they heard back from him, they said. I was beside myself. I knew they used the Red Car Grill as the bar where they made the drinks, and that was in my town of Los Angeles. Surely while waiting for a call back, I could find these bitters at some local distributor. No such luck. After 15 phone calls and false leads, I had gotten nowhere. And no return call either. I decided to do something daring. I figured, if anyone would know who made orange bitters, it was their competition. I put in a call to Angostura International in Trinidad. When I asked my question, I was put on hold and shortly, Clive Cook, director of Angostura was on the line! Embarrassedly, I explained my quest. Did he know of a bitters competitor making *orange* bitters? He graciously responded that Angostura recommended muddling orange peel and Angostura. I smiled and said I'd try it, but I really wanted to find the bottled product. He referred me to his North American counterpart, Jack Margetts, who amicably after a minimum of beating around the bush, said it was true, there was such a company. . .Fee Brothers, in Rochester, NY. "Thank you!" I cried, and called Fee Brothers immediately.

After recounting my adventures to the astonished receptionist, she put me on

Circa 1930s

CONTENTS
5 FLUID OZS.

45% ALCOHOL
BY VOLUME

REGANS'

THE COCKTAILIAN'S DELIGHT FOR DRINKS & CULINARY MARVELS

[INGREDIENTS: WATER, ALCOHOL, ORANGE PEEL, HERBS & SPICES

Orange Bitters

No. 6

The Finest
Orange Bitters
for Man or Beast

None Genuine
without this Signature
Gary Regan

THE SAZERAC COMPANY   NEW ORLEANS, LOUISIANA

the phone with John "Jack" Fee, the grandson of the 1864 company's founder. Not only did they make orange bitters, mainly for regional trade in the Northeast, but they also made genuine pomegranate grenadine, simple syrup, and orgeat syrup. I placed my order on the spot. To illustrate how uncommon this order was for them, they said the only way they were set up to accept payment from me was 30 days net. They'd send out my order, and I had 30 days to pay them! The punch line to this story is that, after I got off the phone with Jack Fee, I received a return call from Philip Collins's publisher. What had he and Ryan done for orange bitters? They'd muddled orange peel in Angostura because they had no more idea where to get the real thing than I did! I began promoting Fee Brothers far and wide to anyone interested in classic cocktails and when I became the spirits maven for the America Online Food & Drink boards, I broadcast their praises nationally and later internationally.

By the way, I am thrilled to be able to say as I did describing the Calvados Cocktail, "depending on the brand of orange bitters you choose. . ."

because by the time this book is released, a second brand of orange bitters should also be on the market. Regans's Orange Bitters #6 is being produced by the Sazerac Company from a formula by my dear friends Gary and Mardee Regan. I know their bitters will be wonderful because I have a handmade batch of their experimental Orange Bitters #4 in my fridge right now, and Gary says they have only gotten better.

The Moscow Mule

⚜

Squeeze ½ of a lime into a Moscow Mule mug
Drop the spent lime shell into the mug.
Add ice cubes and 2 ounces (½ gill, 6 cl) vodka.
Fill with ginger beer

⚜

This drink is a good example of cocktail creep. Anyone today would call the Moscow Mule a cocktail, though it is served on the rocks and, traditionally, in a copper mug. It is more correctly a vodka buck or a highball, themselves both considered cocktail forms today. The oft-told story of the Mule is one of the grand mainstays of cocktail history—and one of the few that involve vodka.

Although the Moscow Mule was not the first vodka drink, it *was* the drink that popularized the spirit with the general public. It combined three nonstarters: vodka, ginger beer (which is what ginger ale was like in the nineteenth century. . .gingery and spicy), and a clunky copper mug that nobody wanted. Vodka had been around since before Prohibition as an import, selling mainly to Eastern Europeans who drank it straight. Most Americans regarded it, if they'd ever heard of it, like aquavit or kvas; interesting, but what do I DO with it? Most recipes previous to the Mule combined it with gin to no apparent purpose. As such, it always fell flat.

Right after Prohibition in 1934, Rudolf "Ralph" Kunetchansky "Kunett" secured rights from friend Vladimir Smirnov (exiled from Russia to France by the Bolshevik revolution) to produce his family's vodka (albeit under the French spelling of his dad Piotr's name) in America. So began Pierre Smirnoff Vodka to no great acclaim. In fact,

Kunett was losing his shirt and in 1939, John Martin, an executive for Heublein, famous in the drink world for their bottled Club Cocktails, agreed to buy the brand and keep Kunett on as an account executive. Heublein was a smart company, but they fared no better until a moment of sublime synchronicity helped them along.

Martin was at the Cock 'n Bull Tavern in Los Angeles with owner and friend Jack Morgan. Morgan had the ginger beer and not much idea what to do with it. A girlfriend of Morgan's had inherited a business that made copper goods (thus the cups) and the

THESE SMIRNOFF DRINKS CHANGED THE DRINKING HABITS OF AMERICA. Unheard of ten years ago, the vodka drinks shown above are household words today. Almost everyone who drinks at all enjoys them. It all began when people suddenly discovered that Smirnoff is the perfect drink ingredient . . . smooth, self-effacing, without liquor taste. It made the good old drinks taste better and inspired delicious new ones! It's smart to drink Smirnoff . . . in more ways than one!

it leaves you breathless

Smirnoff THE GREATEST NAME in VODKA

80 AND 100 PROOF. DISTILLED FROM GRAIN. STE. PIERRE SMIRNOFF FLS. (DIV. OF HEUBLEIN), HARTFORD, CONN.

1950

convergence of these three disparate losing elements, by way of a vodka version of the Gin Buck, was more than the sum of its parts. The Moscow Mule was born. Signature cup, stealthy vodka masquerading as lime-and-ginger (yet still with an unexpected wallop) and spicy, biting ginger beer. In retrospect it was genius. Los Angeles was hot. The new drink could hardly have been more refreshing and fresh tasting or the copper mugs any colder. Zing zing zing!

The drink first became a hit in Los Angeles, then across the country, taking vodka along for the ride. Suddenly vodka was becoming *very* popular; eventually the most popular spirit in the world. With this as its launching pad, people wondered what else they could do with vodka. Let's take the venerable (if awful) Orange Blossom and substitute vodka for the gin. Now we have a Screwdriver. Some tell a probably apocryphal tale of construction workers swizzling that beverage with screwdrivers, hence the name, but that's another story. People looked back beyond all those bad vodka drinks and redis-covered the Red Snapper, a drink created during Prohibition by Ferdinand "Pete" Petiot in 1925 at Harry's American Bar in Paris. It got its name because they worried the original title would be offensive: the Bloody Mary. At the time, American drinkers and writers alike hated it, but some say the lack of American vodka led to the use of gin in it, so what's not to hate? Anyway, from the standpoint of the Moscow Mule, it didn't look so bad, and now there was vodka a-plenty.

So what happened to the Moscow Mule? Two things. First, ginger beer really never did catch on beyond its use in the Mule. (More's the pity, a Gin Buck made with fresh lime, Boodles Gin, and spicy ginger beer is great. So is, amazingly enough, the Mamie Taylor: scotch and ginger beer—*way* better than with bland old ginger ale.) Second, the mugs walked out the door all the time. Therefore bar owners hated 'em, and that was pretty much the end of that. Still, they make a fine and memorable beverage, though ironi-cally, all that's left of the original Cock 'n Bull is the ginger beer bearing its name.

DRINK NOTES

Now though there is still a Cock 'n Bull–branded ginger beer, there are some spicier ones of good quality from Jamaica. My favorite, though is made in exotic South Carolina by a concern named Blenheim Bottlers, owned by the same folks who run that ubiquitous East Coast theme park, South of the Border. These are good people, and the Blenheim Ginger Ale brand dates back to 1903. Know what? Their Old #3 Ginger Ale is hotter than their ginger beer. How hot? If you sniff the opened bottle, you'll sneeze. I'll pass along their address in the back of the book. Also, of course, you don't *have* to use copper mugs for this drink. A double-rocks glass, a collins glass, or its shorter brother the highball glass will work. If you do want to serve them in the historically accurate manner, the mugs show up on eBay all the time.

The Communist

1 ounce (¼ gill, 3 cl) gin
1 ounce (¼ gill, 3 cl) orange juice
½ ounce (⅛ gill, 1.5 cl) cherry brandy
¾ ounce (⅙ gill, 2 cl) fresh lemon juice

Shake in an iced cocktail shaker, and strain into a cocktail glass.

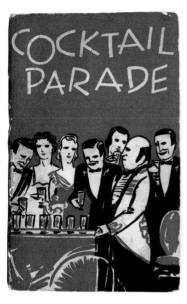

This enjoyable number with the unforgettable name derived from a crude and otherwise quite forgettable cocktail pamphlet from 1933 titled *Cocktail Parade*. As photographers say, though, it just takes one picture.

Gordon's gin circa 1917;
cherry brandy circa 1934

The Fogcutter

1 ounce (¼ gill, 3 cl) white rum
½ ounce (⅛ gill, 1.5 cl) gin
½ ounce (⅛ gill, 1.5 cl) brandy
½ ounce (⅛ gill, 1.5 cl) sweet-and-sour mix (Yes, I know I said no sweet-and-sour mix, but if Tony Ramos mixes the Fogcutter this way, I bow to his experience in this matter.)
2 dashes simple syrup

Combine with ice and blend. Pour into a goblet. Add a float of cherry-flavored brandy on top, and serve.

This recipe fairly closely follows the recipe Trader Vic laid down and subsequent variations created by others thereafter. The key difference appears to be the cherry-flavored brandy float, which is not duplicated elsewhere.

Sven Kirsten, astute academic and foremost archivist of the tiki style, submits the best lost drink he knows: "I really miss that Fogcutter mixed by Tony Ramos at Madame Wu's. Nobody made it like that. . .and I would not know how to train someone in it; it was Tony's secret."

Tony was an original bartender at Don the Beachcomber, and before that mixed at the China Trader. He now holds court on certain days of the week at Cuidad, an upscale restaurant in downtown Los Angeles. Cuidad has simply no idea who they have behind the stick. If anything, it is an understatement to say Mr. Ramos is the finest tropical barman alive today.

The Fogcutter drink appears to be a Trader Vic invention (at least it appeared in his 1947 bar guide), though Tony remembers it from a place in Hollywood, Edna Fogcutter's, at La Brea and Hollywood Boulevards, where it was the signature drink. Whoever gave birth to the Fogcutter, named for a type of diving knife, created a very early and enduring tiki drink.

I, Dr. Cocktail, brought my resources to bear and was able to extract the special recipe from the inimitable Ramos, published for the first time here.

Fogcutter (Early)

½ ounce (⅛ gill, 1.5 cl) orgeat
2 ounces (½ gill, 6 cl) Bacardi Gold rum
1 ounce (¼ gill, 3 cl) Pisco brandy
½ ounce (⅛ gill, 1.5 cl) Plymouth Gin
½ ounce (⅛ gill, 1.5 cl) Gonzalez Sucis sherry (substitute cream sherry, if necessary)
1 ounce (¼ gill, 3 cl) fresh-squeezed orange juice
2 ounces (½ gill, 6 cl) fresh lemon juice

Shake with ice cubes. Pour into a chimney glass, and add more ice to fill.
Float sherry.

DRINK NOTES

For perspective and ample illustration of how protean these drink formulas are, I am also including here another *very* early Don the Beachcomber Fogcutter recipe, unearthed by Jeff "Beachbum" Berry and Larry Dunn. This makes a *fine* Fogcutter.

Curaçao Punch

In a bar glass or goblet combine:

½ tablespoon sugar (this indulged the major nineteenth century sweet tooth—alter to taste)

2 or 3 dashes fresh lemon juice (more of this can also compensate for the sweetness)

1 ounce (¼ gill, 3 cl) soda water

Dissolve the sugar, and fill a glass with finely shaved or thoroughly crushed ice

Add 1 ounce (¼ gill, 3 cl) brandy (Johnson calls for Martell)

2 ounces (½ gill, 6 cl) of orange Curaçao

1 ounce (¼ gill, 3 cl) Jamaican rum (Dale suggests a full-bodied style of rum. I like Bacardi, 8 year.)

Stir well, and ornament as Liberace might with all the fruit at your disposal.

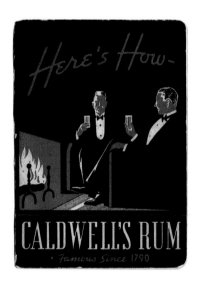

From Harry Johnson's *New and Improved Bartenders Manual* (1882). Dale DeGroff, one of the most famous barmen in the world and author of *The Craft of the Cocktail* (Clarkson Potter, 2002), holds this to be his favorite forgotten potation. ("Forgotten" is used much more strictly by Dale; he has personally revived so many great old drinks.)

Seventh Heaven

1¾ ounces (⁵⁄₁₂ gill, 5 cl) gin
½ ounce (⅛ gill, 1.5 cl) maraschino liqueur
¼ ounce (¹⁄₁₆ gill, 0.75 cl) grapefruit juice
Mint sprig

Shake in an iced cocktail shaker, and strain into a cocktail glass.

This recipe is one of several variations of this once-popular drink. See the La
Floridita Daiquiri (page 76); with rum instead of gin, the Seventh Heaven
becomes a Ribalaigua Daiquiri #3.

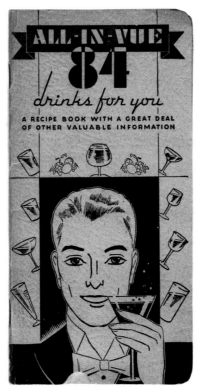

Circa 1930s

The Straits Sling

2 ounces (½ gill, 6 cl) gin
½ ounce (⅛ gill, 1.5 cl) kirschwasser
½ ounce (⅛ gill, 1.5 cl) Bénédictine
Juice of ½ lemon
2 dashes of orange bitters
2 dashes of Angostura bitters

Shake in an iced cocktail shaker. Strain into a sour glass or a Champagne flute. Fill with soda water. Garnish with cherry, orange wheel, lemon twist. . .go crazy. (By the way, if you leave out the soda water and strain the drink into a cocktail glass, it makes a wonderful cocktail—one I call the *Singapore Strait Jacket*.)

The Straits Sling is a drink long forgotten, unlike its famous descendant, the Singapore Sling (page 135). Strictly speaking, the Singapore Sling is no longer a sling at all, insofar as the flavor and composition of that drink form differed from the cocktail. The Singapore Sling, as it has been made since the 1930s, is an individual tropical-styled punch, and is really *the* prototype of the future tiki genre. It is unto itself; a personality drink.

The Straits Sling is, by contrast, a fossil in amber. Perhaps the Singapore Sling came about from a misreading of one original ingredient called for in the Straits

Sling. Combined with the name change, the enhanced drink became sweeter and more romanticized—but a good deal less of a sling. (The "Straits" is still the common way Singapore is known today by its inhabitants, but it has little identification in the wider world.)

Today, to sample the flavor of a traditional sling without undue effort, you have two choices. Buy a bottle of the oh-so-traditional Pimm's Cup #1, which is really a bottled Gin Sling to which only the sparkling constituent, originally soda water, thereafter ginger ale, and now often 7-Up, need be added. Or, for a different, and dare I say fresher, sling flavor, I highly recommend making the recipe featured here.

The probable misapprehension, which led to the radical change in this drink, was over the term "cherry brandy." Generally when cited in bar guides of the era, cherry brandy meant cherry-flavored brandy, a cherry liqueur with a brandy base. The earliest Straits Sling recipe found called for "⅛ gill of Dry Cherry Brandy." Now if it meant a cherry liqueur, "dry" would have no meaning. The driest cherry liqueur would have to be maraschino, and since he mentioned that ingredient by name repeatedly in the book, it is certain he didn't mean that. On the other hand, "dry cherry brandy" takes on a definite meaning if he meant an eau de vie—a literal distillate of cherries—which is unquestionably dry. In fact, there isn't anything sweet about it. Using cherry-flavored brandy in the drink approaches something akin to the Singapore Sling we know now, but using kirschwasser is a revelation. Suddenly, there is the spicy piquant flavor of colonial Singapore in at the end of the Victorian era.

Most of us grew up with a Singapore Sling, which was fruity, red, sweet, and festive. The Singapore Sling transcended its category, and the sling category today would be dead without it. If the original version cannot replace the Personality Drink that the Singapore Sling became so long ago, at least it is a rich sample of its history.

Grant's gin circa 1940; Field's orange bitters (said to be the finest ever made) circa 1930; Benedictine circa 1917; Jung & Wulff (Aromatic) Cocktail Bitters circa 1934; kirsch circa 1960; Clicquot Club soda water circa 1950

The Rose

2 ounces (½ gill, 6 cl) dry French vermouth
1 ounce (¼ gill, 3 cl) kirschwasser
1 teaspoon raspberry syrup

Shake in an iced cocktail shaker, and strain into a chilled cocktail glass. Garnish with maraschino cherry.

From the Chatham Hotel—Paris, 1920. David Wondrich, the formidable cocktail guru for *Esquire* magazine, gives this iteration of the Rose his vote for most lamentably forgotten cocktail.

Have a Heart Cocktail

1½ ounce (⅓ gill, 4.5 cl) gin
¾ ounce (⅙ gill, 2 cl) Swedish Punsch
¾ ounce (⅙ gill, 2 cl) fresh lime juice
¼ ounce (1/16 gill, 0.75 cl) real pomegranate grenadine

Shake in an iced cocktail shaker, and strain into a cocktail glass. Garnish with a lime wedge.

Bad name, good drink. This is a lot like some variations on the Doctor Cocktail. I've had 'em all.

Royal Bermuda Yacht Club Cocktail

※

2 ounces (½ gill, 6 cl) Barbados rum
¾ ounce (⅙ gill, 2 cl) fresh lime juice
2 dashes Cointreau
2 teaspoons Falernum

Shake in an iced cocktail shaker, and strain into a cocktail glass.

※

The Royal Bermuda Yacht Club was established in 1844, largely by officers in the British Army 20th Regiment, stationed in Bermuda. It is one of the three oldest clubs with a Royal Warrant outside the British Isles.

The drink is a very simple and early example of Trader Vic's burgeoning tropics-oriented (but yet to be tiki) repertoire. It is a small cocktail and ought to be kept that way.

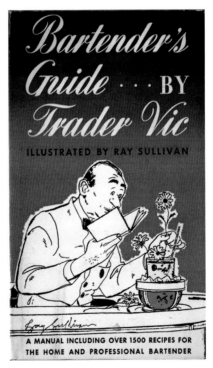

1947

The Vesper

3 ounces (¾ gill, 9 cl) London dry gin (Fleming specified Gordon's, but British
Gordon's is not available in the States. The closest would be Tanqueray, but I
like Boodles, named for the London Men's club of which Fleming was a member.)

1 ounce (¼ gill, 3 cl) vodka (Bond didn't indicate a preference, here, but in later
books he preferred Russian or Polish vodka. Stolichnaya Cristall works well.)

½ ounce (⅛ gill, 1.5 cl) Kina Lillet aperitif (In later years, the company dropped
the "Kina," and the product is now named simply Lillet. Caution! As with
Dubonnet, there are red and white versions; the white is called for.)

A large swathe of lemon peel

Shake in an iced cocktail shaker. Strain into a stemmed cocktail glass. Twist a large
lemon peel over the surface of the drink to garnish.

Although the Great Unwashed will nod knowingly and growl at you, "Of course. It's 007's Vodka Martini—shaken, not stirred," they know not whereof they speak. It is true, though, that when you think of the Vesper, James Bond is right there.

The first Bond book was *Casino Royale*. It was a straight-ahead adventure in keeping with all the books that would follow—and had little in common with the swinging Peter Sellers–David Niven movie that spoofed the wildly popular Sean Connery 007 films. Author Ian Fleming had Bond name the Vesper for love interest Vesper Lynd, later doomed as a double agent. Alas, in the literary sense, the drink was doomed with the woman. The misogynistic young Bond's last words in the book were "The bitch is dead now," and he never drank another Vesper.

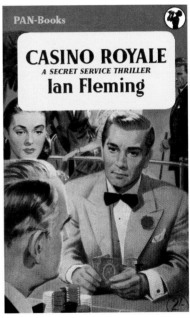

1955; Thanks to www.tikit.net

DRINK NOTES

In actuality, Ian Fleming's favorite bartender created the drink, and it was a work of genius. Just enough vodka to smooth out the sharpness of the gin, and in lieu of the gamey flavor of vermouth, he used a light quinquina (pronounced ken-keena)—a quinine, spice, fruit and spirit-fortified wine—by the name of Kina (think quina) Lillet. This aperitif was smoother, slightly sweeter, and more flavorful than most dry vermouths and stands up admirably to the slightly tamed-down gin. A lemon twist spraying its oil onto the surface of the drink made it complete. Fleming liked it so well he had James Bond recite the entire recipe to a bartender at the Casino Royale.

Crimean Cup á la Marmora

For 2:

In a mixing glass, muddle 2 broad slices of lemon peel with a teaspoon of sugar in ½ ounce (⅛ gill, 1.5 cl) of dark Jamaican rum (Myers's works well).

Add 1 ounce (¼ gill, 3 cl) brandy

½ ounce (⅛ gill, 1.5 cl) Maraschino liqueur

½ ounce (⅛ gill, 1.5 cl) Jamaican rum

2 ounces (½ gill, 6 cl) orgeat syrup

½ ounce (⅛ gill, 1.5 cl) lemon juice

4 ounces (1 gill, 12 cl) soda water in a pitcher

Stir vigorously, and pour into a goblet with 2 or 3 large lumps of ice. Add 3 ounces (¾ gill, 9 cl) chilled Champagne.

From the first mixed drink manual ever, *The Bar-Tender's Guide* by Jerry Thomas (1862).

DRINK NOTES

This recipe was a reduction in quantity from the original (which made enough for 30 people)—the Crimean Cup was meant as a punch. In keeping with the punch theme, a paper-thin sliced lemon wheel floating on the surface of the drink would make an appropriate garnish.

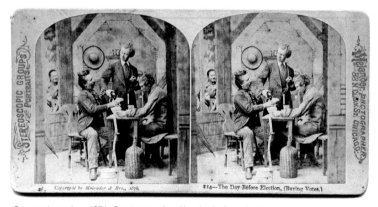

Stereopticon view, 1876. Caption reads: "The day before election, (buying votes.)"

Vowel Cocktail

‎⁂

1 ounce (¼ gill, 3 cl) scotch
1 ounce (¼ gill, 3 cl) sweet vermouth
½ ounce (⅛ gill, 1.5 cl) orange juice (preferably fresh squeezed)
1½ ounces (⅓ gill, 4.5 cl) kummel (Gilka)
1 or 2 dashes Angostura bitters

Shake in an iced cocktail shaker, and strain into a cocktail glass.
(Look for kummel in the Resource Guide, page 137.)

‎⁂

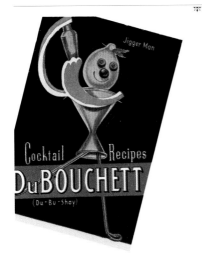

From Barflies and
Cocktails (1927)

Vermouth circa 1933; Ballantine's Scotch
(33 year cask age) bottling circa 1940s;
Gilka kümmel circa 1933. An assortment of
alternative aromatic cocktail bitters are
shown: Litthauer dated 1934; Abbott's circa
1934; Wexmar circa 1936; and
Renault circa 1934

Leatherneck Cocktail

2 ounces (½ gill, 6 cl) blended whiskey
¾ ounce (⅙ gill, 2 cl) blue Curaçao
½ ounce (⅛ gill, 1.5 cl) fresh lime juice

Shake in an iced cocktail shaker, and strain into a cocktail glass. Garnish with a lime wheel.

A *New York World-Telegram* columnist named Frank Farrell apparently invented the Leatherneck. We all know journalists are second only to bartenders when it comes to innovative cocktail creation and consumption. Or perhaps I got the order reversed. Of the drink, Ted Saucier quoted Mr. Farrell: "Shake violently on the rocks and serve in a cocktail glass. . . Stop smoking. Fasten your seat belts. Empty your fountain pens. Because after two gulps, you'll seriously consider yourself capable of straightening out Chinese fire drills." I simply say, it's an odd drink of an odd color. The recipe is from *Bottoms Up* by Ted Saucier (1951).

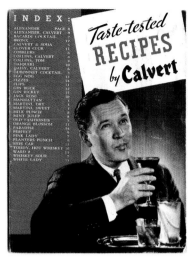

Circa 1935

DRINK NOTES

I rarely, *rarely* use blended whiskey. I don't like it very much, but here it works. Have a dusty old bottle of Crown Royal, Seagram's 7 Crown, or Canadian Club hanging around? Use that.

Lucien Gaudin Cocktail

1 ounce (¼ gill, 3 cl) gin
½ ounce (⅛ gill, 1.5 cl) Cointreau
½ ounce (⅛ gill, 1.5 cl) Campari
½ ounce (⅛ gill, 1.5 cl) dry vermouth

Stir in a mixing glass with ice, and strain into a cocktail glass. Garnish with an orange twist.

This libation is named for the extraordinary fencer who competed in the Olympics in 1920, 1924, and 1928, receiving gold medals in '24 and '28. It is, therefore, a very mature Prohibition cocktail.

Milk Punch

1 ounce (¼ gill, 3 cl) brandy
½ ounce (⅛ gill, 1.5 cl) dark rum
2 teaspoons simple syrup
2 dashes vanilla extract
4 ounces (1 gill, 12 cl) whole milk

Served, traditionally, in a tumbler on shaved ice. Shaved ice was more like snow than crushed ice, but if you pound your ice to smithereens, it'll be similar enough. Grate or shake some nutmeg on top.

Miraculously, you can still walk into a number of New Orleans venues and order this artifact from the first mixed drink guide ever published in 1862. The usual accepted version consists of brandy, simple syrup, vanilla extract, and milk, shaken and strained into a tumbler.

The original version, however, had no vanilla, but it *did* add Virgin Islands rum, and rum often did include a vanilla flavoring component. It also had a dash of water and a tablespoon of sugar—hence simple syrup on the fly.

I love the NOLA version, but saw no reason we couldn't have tradition and technical improvements as well!

Trader Vic Rock Candy Syrup circa 1947; Wray & Nephew 3 Dagger Jamaica Rum circa 1940; Ramona (California) brandy distilled 1917 and bottled 1930. The stereopticon view is dated 1870.

DRINK NOTES

Like the Coffee Cocktail (page 50), this is usually a morning potation. Latter-day New Orleans recipes offer a variation with bourbon, but not for *this* Doctor.

Don the Beachcomber's Zombie

1 ounce (¼ gill, 3 cl) unsweetened pineapple juice
1 ounce (¼ gill, 3 cl) fresh lemon juice
1 ounce (¼ gill, 3 cl) fresh lime juice
1 ounce (¼ gill, 3 cl) passion fruit syrup
1 teaspoon brown sugar
1 dash Angostura bitters
1 ounce (¼ gill, 3 cl) gold Puerto Rican rum
1 ounce (¼ gill, 3 cl) 151 proof Demerara rum (from Guyana)
1 ounce (¼ gill, 3 cl) white Puerto Rican rum

Dissolve the brown sugar in the lemon juice. Combine it with everything else in a cocktail shaker with crushed ice. Shake well, and pour it all into a collins glass. Garnish with a mint sprig.

This most quintessential of tiki drinks gets Jeff "Beachbum" Berry's vote for greatest forgotten drink. The Bum is unquestionably the greatest living authority on classic Polynesian-themed drinks. He is also the author of *Beachbum Berry's Grog Log* (SLG Publishing, 1998) and *Intoxica* (2002), both bibles to tiki drink admirers. I can do no better than to quote the Beachbum from *Intoxica*:

> "We felt like Bouchard discovering the Rosetta Stone when we found this one. Don's Zombie was his most infamous invention, which went on to become the most legendary unsolved mystery in the annals of the tropical drink. Even Don's own bartenders didn't know how to make it: they poured the ingredients from bottles marked only by numbers or letters, the right combination of which was the sole part of the code they knew. . .This particular formula was contributed by Don the Beachcomber himself to a 1950 barbecue manual written and self-published in a three-ring binder by his friend Louis Spievak. Far be it from us to doubt its authenticity, especially after reading the caveat Don appended to it: 'I originated and have served this 'thing' since 1934. . . anyone that says otherwise is a liar!! Signed: DON.'"

Berry put it to me this way: "In 10 years of researching tropical drinks, I don't think I've ever come across a better one than Don the Beachcomber's Zombie. Not the cough syrup or kool ade poured in even the toniest bars I've been to, but the original recipe I finally managed to unearth. It's strong, yet not too alcoholic, neither too sweet nor too tart, with a layered, complex taste that changes like a long sunset from first sip to last. Over the years, the Zombie has suffered a lot of abuse by authors of cocktail guides (notably Gavin Duffy, who practically radiated contempt for the drink in his books), but I believe that's only because they never sampled the original, just the various abominations Don's imitators have foisted on the public since his passing (and, no doubt, during his heyday too). I used to be one of those authors myself—although I've scoured hundreds of recipe books, I never saw a zombie recipe I liked until I found this one."

I wish I had either the depth of understanding (or the taste buds) of Jeff Berry when it comes to these tropical punches. As it is, I just follow him around and happily drink what he tells me to.

1942

GREAT OLD STANDARDS

In the discussion of the forgotten cocktails in this book, several classic standard cocktails have been mentioned. Here are recipes for them, included for the sake of comparison.

THE BLOODY MARY

2 ounces (½ gill, 6 cl) vodka

6 ounces (1½ gill, 18 cl) tomato juice or V-8

2 dashes Worcestershire sauce

1 dash Tabasco sauce

Stir all together in iced highball glass. Sprinkle celery salt on top. Garnish with a celery stalk.

CHAMPAGNE COCKTAIL

In either a tall (pretty) Champagne flute or a saucer (traditional) Champagne glass:

1 sugar cube

4 dashes Angostura bitters

Fill with champagne. Garnish with a lemon twist.

CUBA LIBRÉ

In an iced highball glass combine:

2 ounces (½ gill, 6 cl) rum (Cuban if you can get it, or Brugal Dominican rum, or the rum of your choice)

Juice of ½ fresh lime

Fill with Coca Cola. Garnish with a lime wedge.

The trick, here, is that this drink is not "just a rum and Coke." The lime juice changes everything. Cola is under utilized in general drink creation. See the Filmograph Cocktail, page 72.

THE GIMLET

An immortal old film noir drink, traditionally made with gin and Rose's Lime Juice Cordial. This is FAR to sweet for me, so I combined the recipes for the Gimlet with that of the Gin Rickey:

2½ ounces (⅝ gill, 7.5 cl) gin or vodka

½ ounce (⅛ gill, 1.5 cl) Rose's Lime Juice Cordial

½ ounce (⅛ gill, 1.5 cl) fresh lime juice

Combine in an iced cocktail shaker. Shake, and strain into a cocktail glass.

THE MANHATTAN

Along with the Champagne Cocktail, the oldest cocktail still made exactly the same way it was 145 years ago.

2½ (⅝ gill, 7.5 cl) ounces rye or Bourbon

1 ounce (¼ gill, 3 cl) sweet vermouth (or, for a so-called Perfect Manhattan ½ ounce [⅛ gill, 1.5 cl] each dry and sweet vermouth, with a tip of the hat to Bob "Magoo" McCarthy)

2 dashes Angostura bitters

Combine in an iced mixing glass. Stir, and strain into a cocktail glass, or strain onto fresh rocks in a rocks glass. Either way, garnish with a cherry or a twist, or both.

THE ORIGINAL MARGARITA

1½ ounces (⅓ gill, 4.5 cl) reposado tequila

1½ ounces (⅓ gill, 4.5 cl) Cointreau

1½ ounces (⅓ gill, 4.5 cl) fresh lime juice

Shake in an iced cocktail shaker. Strain into a large cocktail glass, rim crusted with salt.

CLASSIC 1950s MARTINI

3 ounces (¾ gill, 9 cl) gin or vodka

½ ounce (⅛ gill, 1.5 cl) dry vermouth

Stir vigorously and long in an iced Martini pitcher. Add a dash of orange bitters. Garnish with a pimento-stuffed olive or a lemon twist.

For the more recent variety, try 3½ ounces (⅞ gill, 10.5 cl) gin or vodka and a dash of dry vermouth. Shake, strain and add garnish of choice. (Note: gin is more tolerant of vermouth than vodka.)

THE NEGRONI

1 ounce (¼ gill, 3 cl) gin or vodka

1 ounce (¼ gill, 3 cl) sweet vermouth

1 ounce (¼ gill, 3 cl) Campari

Stir vigorously in an iced mixing glass. Strain into a small cocktail glass. Garnish with orange wheel.

OLD-FASHIONED

Lots of fights occur over this drink. It started its life as a simple Whiskey Cocktail in the first bar guides and contained simply rye whiskey, bitters, perhaps a dash of Curaçao, enough water to dissolve sugar, and sugar. Latter-day guides took to calling it the "Old-Fashioned Whiskey Cocktail," and some of them discarded the Curaçao, allowing for a piece of sometimes-muddled orange peel. As the years wore on, it morphed into a veritable fruit cocktail with oranges, orange juice, cherries, and sometimes a piece of pineapple—oft times all mushed together, or shaken together with blended whiskey. Either way, this final evolution created an ugly slurry that has nothing to do with the original drink.

Dr. Cocktail hereby announces: Henceforth, the last version will never again be served! The second version, with 2 dashes of bitters, ½ teaspoon of sugar, a few drops of water, and a lone broad swathe of the orange peel ONLY, muddled to express the orange oil, and combined with good rye or Bourbon—his drink is henceforth known EXCLUSIVELY as the **Old-Fashioned**.

The original version, rye whiskey, sugar, drops of water, bitters—with or without Curaçao—this drink is now remembered as the **Whiskey Cocktail**. Both drinks are served on a lump or two of ice in an old-fashioned glass. I have spoken.

See? World peace can be that easy

PIMM'S CUP

In an iced highball glass combine:

2 ounces (½ gill, 6 cl) Pimm's #1 Gin Sling

Fill with 7-Up if you're modern, Bitter lemon or lemonade if you're British, or Ginger Ale (or ginger beer) if you're a time traveler like I am.

Stir. Garnish with a long wedge of cucumber, and breathe deep as you sip.

THE ROB ROY

2½ ounces (⅝ gill, 7.5 cl) Scotch

1 ounce (¼ gill, 3 cl) sweet vermouth (or more for a sweeter drink)

2 dashes Angostura bitters

Combine in iced mixing glass. Stir, and strain into a cocktail glass or onto fresh rocks in a rocks glass. Either way, garnish with a cherry.

RUSTY NAIL

2 ounces (½ gill, 6 cl) good smoky Scotch

1 ounce (¼ gill, 3 cl) Drambuie Liqueur

Combine in a small rocks glass on a couple lumps of ice and swizzle. Garnish with a lemon twist.

THE SAZERAC

3 ounces (¾ gill, 9 cl) rye whiskey (Old Overholt is fine, or a fancier brand)

1 teaspoon of simple syrup (or more to taste)

3 to 4 dashes Peychaud's bitters

1 teaspoon of Herbsaint, or Pernod, or other pastis

1 strip of lemon peel

Chill an Old-Fashioned glass. Coat the inside of the glass with the pastis, leaving a small puddle in the bottom. In an iced mixing glass, combine the whiskey and the simple syrup and stir. Strain contents into the glass. Smartly twist the lemon peel over the surface of the drink and discard. Serve.

THE SIDECAR

As originally made.

1 ounce (¼ gill, 3 cl) brandy

1 ounce (¼ gill, 3 cl) Cointreau

1 ounce (¼ gill, 3 cl) fresh lemon juice

Combine in iced cocktail shaker. Shake, and strain into a cocktail glass. The beauty of this cocktail is that if it is too strong you just decrease the brandy. Too sweet? Add more lemon. Too sour? Add more Cointreau. It's a comfortably adjustable drink!

THE SINGAPORE SLING

2 ounces (½ gill, 6 cl) gin

¾ ounce (⅙ gill, 2 cl) Cherry Heering (or other cherry-flavored brandy)

2 teaspoons Bénédictine

2 teaspoons Cointreau

2 ounces (½ gill, 6 cl) pineapple juice

¾ ounce (⅙ gill, 2 cl) fresh lime juice

2 dashes of real pomegranate grenadine

1 dash Angostura bitters

Combine in an iced cocktail shaker. Shake, and strain into highball or collins glass with a couple lumps of ice. Top with soda water. Garnish with cherry, pineapple, and orange.

TOM COLLINS

2 ounce (½ gill, 6 cl) gin

1 ounce (¼ gill, 3 cl) fresh lemon juice

1 ounce (¼ gill, 3 cl) simple syrup

Combine in an iced cocktail shaker.

Shake, and strain into highball or collins glass with 2 or 3 lumps of ice. Top with soda water. Garnish with cherry and orange.

WHISKEY SOUR

2 ounces (½ gill, 6 cl) bourbon or rye whiskey

1 ounce (¼ gill, 3 cl) fresh lemon juice

¾ ounce (⅙ gill, 2 cl) simple syrup

Combine in an iced cocktail shaker.

Shake, and strain into a 6-ounce (1½ gill, 18 cl) sour glass. Top with soda water. Garnish with cherry and lemon.

RESOURCE GUIDE

Absinthe: www.macha-weine.de

Amer Picon: Proprietary French bittersweet spirit-based aperitif beverage bitters. Notable in the Basque drink, the Picon Punch. Substitute: Torani Amer. www.bevmo.com

Applejack or Apple Jack: Generic for American apple distillate often (but not necessarily) blended with neutral spirits. Brands: Laird's and Captain Applejack. www.bevmo.com

Boker's Bitters: Defunct proprietary New York–based digestive bitters brand called for in nineteenth century cocktail guides as aromatic bitters. No evidence after the turn-of-the-century. Boker's Bitters Formula below researched and reconstructed by Dr. Cocktail from the formula found in *The Scientific American Cyclopedia of Receipts, Notes & Queries* 1898)

¾ ounce (⅙ gill, 2 cl) quassia chips
¾ ounce (⅙ gill, 2 cl) powdered catechu
½ ounce (⅛ gill, 1.5 cl) cardamom
1 ounce (¼ gill, 3 cl) dried orange peel
Macerate for 10 days in 1 quart (8 gills, 96 cl) strong whiskey. Filter and add 1 gallon (32 gills, 384 cl) of water. Color with Mallow or Malva flowers.

Uncommon Ingredient Sources for Boker's Bitters:
Quassia & Malva Flowers:
CedarVale Natural Health
P.O. Box 575
607 Crocker St.
Cedar Vale, KS 67024 USA
866-758-1012
www.cedarvale.net

Catechu:
Alchemy Works
3074 Lake Rd.,
Horseheads, NY 14845-3102 USA
607-737-9250
www.alchemyworks.com/herb_catechu.html

Dried orange peel:
Spices Etc.
P.O. Box 2088
Savannah, GA 31402-2088 USA
800-827-6373
www.spicesetc.com

Brugal rum: www.internetwines.com

Calvados: Aged apple brandy from the Calvados/Normandy region of France. www.bevmo.com or www.internetwines.com

Chartreuse: Proprietary French multiherbal, high-proof, monastic liqueur in green and yellow varieties. www.internetwines.com

Cherry Heering: Proprietary Danish cherry liqueur with brandy base. Sometimes called Peter Heering after its creator. www.hitimewine.net or www.internetwines.com or www.bevmo.com

Cuban Rum: Main brand, Havana Club. www.eBay.com or www.macha-weine.de in Germany. (He ships and speaks English.)

Demerara rum, 151 proof/151-proof: Generic for rums from the island of Guyana and made with Demerara sugar. The only acceptable 151 rum. Brand available: Lemonhart. www.internetwines.com

Falernum: Syrup, lightly alcoholic (5% to 6%), used almost exclusively in rum-based tropical drinks. Thick, translucent, and lightly golden in color, it has a sweet ,subtle, and complex character. Fee Bros. 800-961-3337 www.feebrothers.com

Genever gin: Generic for Dutch/German aromatic pot still distillate of fermented juniper berries, grain, and other botanicals in wood-aged and unaged varieties. Quite a bit more character than London Dry Gin. www.bevmo.com

Gilka Kummel: Best proprietary brand of grain-neutral-spirit-based, caraway-flavored liqueur from Northern Europe. www.internetwines.com or www.bevmo.com

Ginger beer: Generic for carbonated, sweetened soda, generally a spicier more heavily ginger-flavored version of ginger ale; usually nonalcoholic, though some historical versions were, in fact, flavored, fermented, alcoholic beer. Blenheim's Ginger Ale and Ginger Beers are highly recommended. www.sodapopstop.com

Grenadine: Generic for red or purple syrup sweetener and colorant made from pomegranate juice and/or artificial flavorings. Usually nonalcoholic. Brands containing real pomegranate are most desirable. Two such are Angostura and Fee Brothers American Beauty. Fee Brothers American Beauty Pomegranate Grenadine is highly recommended. www.feebrothers.com

Kirschwasser or Kirsch: Generic for traditionally French, German, or Swiss unsweetened, unaged cherry eau de vie. Now it is produced globally. www.bevmo.com or www.internetwines.com

Kola Tonic: lekker.safeshopper.com or RSA-Overseas.com, LLC
9225 Vernon Drive
Great Falls, VA 22066 USA
703-757-9432

Kummel: Generic for grain-neutral-spirit-based caraway-flavored liqueur from Northern Europe. Brand example: Gilka Kummel. www.bevmo.com

Lillet Blanc: Proprietary French quinquina with slightly orange character. www.internetwines.com

Maraschino liqueur: Generic for clear liqueur flavored with crushed Dalmation Marasca cherries and the pits, stems, and seeds deriving therefrom. www.internetwines.com or www.bevmo.com

Orange bitters: Generic for concentrated bitter tincture of orange peel, spices, herbs, and spirits. Example: Fee Bros. Orange Bitters. With any luck by the time you have this book, Regan's Orange Bitters #6 will also be available from Sazerac. Fee Bros. 800-961-3337 www.feebrothers.com, Sazerac www.sazerac.com or www.buffalotrace.com/giftshop.asp.

Orange Curaçao: Generic for orange liqueur made in various colors but similar in flavor to one another, in neutral spirit base. Quality varies widely between domestic and imported varieties. The best are made from real Curaçao oranges. Best brand in the United States is Marie Brizard. Far better still is Bardinet Curaçao, which can be surprisingly inexpensive when ordered internationally. www.macha-weine.de

Orgeat: Generic syrup of almonds, orange flower water, and sometimes barley water; often used in tropical and other cocktails. Now always nonalcoholic, it was once made with a small quantity of brandy. Light tan in color. Fee Bros. 800-961-3337 www.feebrothers.com or www.bevmo.com

Parfait Amour: Generic for once-popular nineteenth century liqueur of spices, vanilla, orange, and flowers. Once again somewhat more available than previously, thanks to the distribution efforts of Marie Brizard, whom we believe to be the sole current manufacturer of this product in the United States since Bols suspended production here. Notable in the Jupiter Cocktail. www.bevmo.com or www.internetwines.com

Passion fruit juice or nectar:
RSA-Overseas.com, LLC
9225 Vernon Drive
Great Falls, VA 22066 USA
703-757-9432. www.kitchenetc.com, www.naturesflavors.com, and www.carribeansupplies.com

Passion fruit syrup: www.tradervics.com

Peychaud bitters: Proprietary Louisiana brand of aromatic bitters. Produced since the nineteenth century, currently by Sazerac. Notable and essential in the Sazerac cocktail. www.internetwines.com

Plymouth gin: Proprietary dry gin from Plymouth, England, of different character than London Dry. Mild and pleasant. Available in different proofs. Particularly noted in the Pink Gin. www.bevmo.com

Raspberry syrup: There are many raspberry syrups available. My secret (don't tell!) is that I use Smucker's Red Raspberry Syrup, an elegant natural fruit syrup. It'll transform your cocktails. Unfortunately, when ordering from Smuckers you are required to buy six bottles and with shipping you'll pay a ridiculous $26. Mail order sources for single bottles is elusive, but most U.S. supermarkets will cooperate in ordering Smucker's products like this one for you. If you can't find their raspberry syrup in your area, I also recommend Monin Raspberry Syrup. Monin syrups are mainly used as coffee flavorings, but they are extremely well made and work admirably in cocktails. Monin is available nationwide. www.smuckers.com and www.monin.com

Real pomegranate grenadine: Generic for red or purple syrup sweetener and colorant made from pomegranate juice and flavorings. Usually nonalcoholic. Two such are Angostura and Fee Brothers American Beauty. Fee Brothers American Beauty Pomegranate Grenadine is highly recommended. www.feebrothers.com

Rock candy syrup: Generic for high-concentration water and sugar solution, either prepared at home or available commercially. Also called cane syrup, simple syrup, gomme syrup, capillaire syrup, and syrup. www.feebrothers.com

Simple syrup: Generic for high-concentration water and sugar solution, either prepared at home or available commercially. Also called cane syrup, rock candy syrup, gomme syrup, capillaire syrup, and syrup. www.feebrothers.com

Swedish punsch: Generic for a type of smoky Scandinavian liqueur, Batavia Arak/Arrack-based and flavored. Sweetened with cane sugar. Simply put, Swedish punsch is to rum as Drambuie is to scotch. Notable brands are Cederlund's Carlshamn's, and Gronstedt. Like a dark, smoky rum and when added to other lesser rums tends to enhance their value in an estimable way. Grönstedts Blue, Carlshamn's, and Cederlund's are recommended in that order. www.northerner.com Grönstedts is on online page 22. You must get to it manually; the search function will not find it.

Torani Amer: Substitute for Amer Picon. Notable in the Basque drink, the Picon Punch. www.bevmo.com

BIBLIOGRAPHY

Bacchus and Cordon Bleu. *New Guide for the Hotel, Bar, Restaurant, Butler, and Chef.* London: William Nicholson and Sons, 1885.

Baker, Charles H., Jr. *Gentleman's Companion: Around the World with Jigger, Beaker and Flask.* New York: Crown, 1946.

Bar La Florida Cocktails. Havana, Cuba: Bar La Florida, 1934 (Printed by Lloret, Havana, Cuba).

Bergeron, Victor. *Trader Vic's Bartender's Guide.* Garden City, NY: Doubleday and Co., 1972.

Bergeron, Victor. *Bartender's Guide by Trader Vic.* Garden City, NY: Garden City, 1948.

Berry, Jeff. *Beachbum Berry's Intoxica!* Los Angeles, CA: SLG Publishing, 2002.

Berry, Jeff and Annene Kaye. *Beachbum Berry's Grog Log.* Los Angeles, CA: Slave Labor Publications, 1998.

Carling, T.E. *Complete Book of Drink.* London: Philosophical Library, 1952.

Cobb, Irvin. *Irvin Cobb's Own Recipe Book.* Louisville, KY: Frankfort Distilleries, Inc., 1934.

Cock 'n Bull: First Thirty Years. Los Angeles, CA: Cock n' Bull Restaurant, 1967.

Cocktails Bar La Florida. Havana, Cuba: Bar La Florida, 1939.

Cocktail Parade. Scarborough, NY: Canapé Parade, 1933.

Collins, Philip and Sam Sargeant. *The Art of the Cocktail.* San Francisco, CA: Chronicle Books, 1992.

Craddock, Harry. *Savoy Cocktail Book.* New York, NY: Richard R. Smith, 1930.

Dardis, Tom. *The Thirsty Muse: Alcohol and the American Writer.* New York, NY: Ticknor and Fields, Houghton Mifflin Company, 1989.

DeVoto, Bernard. *The Hour.* Boston: Houghton Mifflin Company, 1948.

Duffy, Patrick Gavin. *Official Mixer's Manual.* New York, NY: Ray Long & Richard R. Smith, 1934.

Fleming, Ian. *Casino Royale.* New York, NY: The Macmillan Company, 1953.

Gale, Hyman and Gerald F. Marco. *How and the When.* Chicago, IL: Printed by Lincoln Printing Co., 1937.

Gash, Chas. O. Untitled recipe book. Hand-typed loose-leaf notebook. The Texas Company, 1930s.

Harwell, Richard Barksdale. *The Mint Julep.* Charlottesville, VA: University Press of Virginia, 1975.

Hopkins, Albert A., ed. *Scientific American Cyclopedia of Receipts, Notes and Queries.* New York, NY: Munn and Co., 1898.

Johnson, Harry. *New and Improved Illustrated Bartender's Manual.* New York, NY: Printed by I. Goldmann, New York, NY, 1888.

Jones, Stan. *Jones's Complete Barguide.* Los Angeles, CA: Barguide Enterprises, 1977.

Lord, Tony. *The World Guide to Spirits, Aperitifs, and Cocktails.* New York: Sovereign Books, 1979.

Lowe, Paul E. *Drinks As They Are Mixed.* Chicago, IL: Frederick J. Drake and Co., 1904.

McElhone, Harry. *ABC of Mixing Cocktails.* London: Odham's Press Ltd., 1923.

McElhone, Harry and Wynn McElhone. *Barflies and Cocktails.* Paris: Lecram Press, 1927.

Meier, Frank. *Artistry of Mixing Drinks.* Paris: Fryam Press, 1936.

Noling, A.W. *Beverage Literature: A Bibliography.* Metuchen, NJ: Scarecrow Press, Inc., 1971.

Regan, Gary and Mardee Haidin Regan. *New Classic Cocktails.* New York, NY: Macmillan, 1997

"Robert." *Cocktails: How to Mix Them.* London: Herbert Jenkins Ltd., 1922.

Saucier, Ted. *Ted Saucier's Bottoms Up.* New York, NY: Greystone Press/Hawthorn Books, 1962.

Schmidt, William. *The Flowing Bowl.* New York, NY: Charles L. Webster and Co., 1891.

Schumann, Charles. *Tropical Bar Book.* New York, NY: Stewart, Tabori and Chang, 1989.

Tarling, W.J. *Cafe Royal Cocktail Book.* London: Publications from Pall Mall Ltd., 1937.

Terrington, William. *Cooling Cups and Dainty Drinks.* London: George Routledge and Sons, 1869.

Thomas, Jerry. *Bar-Tender's Guide.* New York: Dick and Fitzgerald, 1887.

Bar-Tender's Guide & Bon Vivant's Companion. New York, NY: Dick and Fitzgerald, 1862.

Townsend, Jack and Tom Moore McBride. *The Bartender's Book.* New York, NY: Viking Press, 1951.

U.K.B.G. Guide to Drinks. London: United Kingdom Bartenders' Guild, 1955.

Visakay, Stephen. *Vintage Bar Ware.* Paducah, KY: Collector Books, 1997.

Weiss, Harry B. *History of Applejack.* Trenton, NJ: New Jersey Agricultural Society, 1954.

ABOUT THE AUTHOR

Ted Haigh, a.k.a. Dr. Cocktail, makes his living as a graphic designer in the Hollywood movie industry and has worked on such spectacles as *O Brother, Where Art Thou?*; *American Beauty*; and *The Insider*. Although he has been diligently researching cocktails since the 1980s, his moonlighting as a cocktail historian became public in 1995 when he hosted the America Online spirits boards. On that stage he made his (odd) reputation and got to know such cocktail greats as Gary and Mardee Regan, Dale "King Cocktail" DeGroff, Martin Doudoroff, William Grimes, David Wondrich, Robert "Drinkboy" Hess, Colin Field, and Audrey "Libation Goddess" Saunders. In the intervening years, he has been quoted and referenced by the *New York Times*, *Esquire*, *The Malt Advocate*, *Men's Journal*, as well as in various books and other media. He is a partner in CocktailDB.com, an encyclopedic database of cocktail knowledge.

AFTERWORD

It was no easy task selecting these few forgotten cocktails from the hundreds more deserving—and the thousands more lacking ANY saving grace. There are hundreds of fascinating bar manuals issued between the time Jerry Thomas's forward-thinking effort hit the street in 1862 and when this backward-thinking book of mine hit the shelves. Each has the potential for creating just one great drink, and although many fell short of even that, others far surpassed their quota. I leave you now, not only with all these drinks to try, but also with a challenge to search out your own. The old guides are waiting for you in book shops and online and, as in *Vintage Spirits & Forgotten Cocktails*, you never know what you'll find.

Cheers,
—Doc

REST-IN-PEACE COCKTAIL INGREDIENTS

The following ingredients are either unavailable to us or completely defunct, invalidating over a hundred years of recipes calling for them. Someday perhaps they can be revived. Until then, just sip and dream.

Abbott's Bitters

Boker's Bitters

Caperitif

Crème Yvette

Forbidden Fruit

Khoosh Bitters

Pimento Liqueur (or Pimento Dram)

Secrestat Bitters

Tonicola

If you are curious about these products, check out www.cocktaildb.com. They are all described there.

The End

INDEX

A

Absinthe, 46
The Alamagoozlum Cocktail, 21–23
The Algonquin Cocktail, 34–35
Applejack, 26–27
The Avenue Cocktail, 36–37
The Aviation, 74

B

Baker, Charles H., Jr., 22
Baldwin, Brooks, 33
Barbara West Cocktail, 29
Barnum (Was Right) Cocktail, 70
Bar-Tender's Guide (Thomas), 11–12, 43, 51, 65
The Bebbo Cocktail, 71
Bergeron, Trader Vic, 77–78
Bergeron, Walter, 48
Berry, Jeff, 130
The Blackthorn Cocktail, 92
The Blinker Cocktail, 93
Blood and Sand, 56–57
The Bloody Mary, 132
Blue Moon, 74
Bourbon, 17–18
The Brandy Crusta, 42–43
Breau, Ted, 46
Bronx Cocktail, 68–69
The Brooklyn Cocktail, 59

C

Café Royal Bar Book, 40, 41
Calvados, 26, 81, 82
The Calvados Cocktail, 100–101
Casino Royale (Fleming), 123
Champagne Cocktail, 132
Chatham Hotel Special, 75
Cherry brandy, 119
Classic 1950s Martini, 133
Clover Club Cocktail, 55
Cobb, Irvin, 64
Cocktails, history of, 10–19
    Prohibition era, 13–15
    Temperance movement, 12–13
The Coffee Cocktail, 50–51
Cognac, 103
Cointreau, 63
The Communist, 112–113
The Corpse Reviver #2, 44–45
Craddock, Harry, 45
Crème de violette, 74
Crème Yvette, 74
Crimean Cup á la Marmora, 124
Cuba Libré, 132
Curaçao, 107
Curaçao Punch, 116

D

Daiquiris, 76–79
    La Floridita Daiquiri, 76–79
DeGroff, Dale, 116
The Delicious Sour, 52–53
The Derby Cocktail, 83
DeVoto, Bernard, 69
Doctor Cocktail, 104–105
Don the Beachcomber's Zombie, 130–131

E

East India Cocktail, 58
Eggs, as ingredient, 21, 50, 52–53, 54–55
Embury, David A., 15, 43

F

Farrell, Frank, 127
Fee Brothers, 108–109
Field, Colin, 103
The Filmograph Cocktail, 72–73
Fleming, Ian, 123
La Floridita Daiquiri, 76–79
The Fogcutter, 114
Fogcutter (Early), 115
Fred Collins Fizz, 28
The French 75, 60–61

G

The Gentleman's Companion (Baker), 22
The Georgia Mint Julep, 64–65
The Gimlet, 132
Gin, 66–67
Ginger beer, 110–111
The Golden Dawn, 38–39
Gomme syrup, 21
Grenadine, 25
Grimes, William, 74

H

Harry's New York Bar, 88, 91
Have a Heart Cocktail, 120
Hemingway, Ernest, 77, 79
Herbal liqueurs, 82
Hess, Robert, 61

I

The Income Tax Cocktail, 68–69
Internet resources, 19

J

Jack Rose Cocktail, 24–27
Johnson, Harry, 81
The Jupiter Cocktail, 30–31

K

Kirsten, Sven, 114
Knickerbocker à la Monsieur, 87
Kola tonic, 73
Kunett, Rudolf "Ralph" Kunetchansky, 110

L

Laird & Co., 27
Leatherneck Cocktail, 126–127
Lillet, 45, 122, 123
Liqueurs, herbal, 82
Lord, Tony, 67
Lucien Gaudin Cocktail, 127

M

Malacca Gin, 66
The Manhattan, 133
Margaritas, 18–19
    The Original Margarita, 133
Martinis, 17
    Classic 1950s Martini, 133
Martin, John, 110
Maurice, 69
McElhone, Harry, 43, 88
Meier, Frank, 105
Milk Punch, 128–129
The Millionaire Cocktail, 84–86
Mint Julep, 64–65
The Modernista, 47
The Monkey Gland, 88–89
Morgan, Jack, 110–111
The Moscow Mule, 110–111
The Mother-In-Law Cocktail, 32–33
Myers, Billy, 89

N

The Negroni, 134

O

Old-Fashioned, 134
Orange bitters, 108–109
The Original Margarita, 133

P

Palm Beach Special, 94
Parfait Amour, 30–31
Park Avenue Cocktail, 95
Pegu Club Cocktail, 96 97
Pendennis Cocktail, 102
Picon Punch, 98–99
Pimm's Cup, 134
Pink Gin, 66–67
Pink Lady, 55
Plymouth Gin, 66

R

Ramos, Tony, 114
Red Snapper, 111
Regan, Gary and Mardee, 41, 62, 109
Reichert, Daniel, 97
Ritz Sidecar, 103
The Rob Roy, 134
The Rose, 120
Royal Bermuda Yacht Club Cocktail, 121
Rusty Nail, 134

S

Santini, Joe, 43
Satan's Whiskers Cocktail, 106–107
Saucier, Ted, 127
The Sazerac, 135
Schmidt, William, 53
Schumann, Charles, 77
The Scoff Law Cocktail, 90–91
Scotch, 17
The Secret Cocktail, 54–55
The Seelbach Cocktail, 62–63
Seger, Adam, 62, 109
Seventh Heaven, 117
The Sidecar, 43, 135. *See also* Ritz Sidecar
The Singapore Sling, 119, 135
Smirnov, Vladimir, 110
Soyer au Champagne, 49
The Straits Sling, 118–119

T

Taggart, Chuck, 48
Thomas, Jerry, 11, 43, 51, 65
Tom Collins, 136
Torani Amer, 99
Triple sec, 63
The Twentieth Century Cocktail, 40–41

U

United Kingdom Bartenders' Guild, 14, 39, 41

V

The Vesper, 122–123
Vieux Carré Cocktail, 48
Vodka, 16, 110–111
Voronoff, Dr. Serge, 89
Vowel Cocktail, 123

W

Whiskey, 15–16, 91
Whiskey Cocktail, 134
Whiskey Sour, 136
The Widow's Kiss, 80–82

Z

Zazarac Cocktail, 33